The seven sacraments

ENTERING THE MYSTERIES OF GOD

STRATFORD CALDECOTT

A Crossroad Book
The Crossroad Publishing Company
New York

The Crossroad Publishing Company
16 Penn Plaza – 481 Eighth Avenue, Suite 1550
New York, NY 10001

Printed in the United States of America

The text of this book is set in 11/14 Cochin.
The display faces are Baskerville and Democratica.

Library of Congress Cataloging-in-Publication Data

Caldecott, Stratford.
    The Seven Sacraments : entering the mysteries of God / Stratford Caldecott.
        p. cm.
    Includes bibliographical references (p.   ) and index.
    ISBN 0-8245-2376-8 (alk. paper)
        1. Sacraments – Catholic Church. 2. Catholic Church – Doctrines.
    I. Title.
    BX2200.C26 2006
    234′.16 – dc22

                                                              2005036034

ISBN 13: 978-0-8245-2376-3

1 2 3 4 5 6 7 8 9 10   12 11 10 09 08 07 06

Just as the human race could not be redeemed unless the Son of God were born of the Virgin, so too the Virgin had to be born from whom the Word was to become flesh. That is, first a house had to be built in which the king of heaven might deign to descend and be a guest. I refer to the house of which God said through Solomon: "Wisdom built herself a house and hewed seven columns for it" (Prov. 9:1). This virginal house rested on seven columns, because the venerable mother of God was endowed with the seven gifts of the Holy Spirit. The bridal chamber had first to be constructed that would receive the bridegroom as he came for his Marriage with holy Church.

— Saint Peter Damian (d. 1072), Homily 45 on Mary

He has transposed the mystery of his Incarnation into each individual believer. And he works from within each one, for into each he has placed the mirror of heaven by means of communion....A mirror of heaven sparkles at one point in the world, undiminished, uncompromising and endowed with the strength to transform man and his whole activity towards heaven. — Adrienne von Speyr

Contents

Contents

A Word from the Author

Some readers may find this book peculiar, and for them a word of explanation may be necessary. I addressed it in part to the many spiritual seekers outside the Catholic Church, who might be curious to learn what Catholicism has to offer them in this day and age. I myself was once such a seeker, who found much that was true, good, and beautiful in other traditions before discovering my spiritual home within Christianity. Accordingly, I have written his book as a signpost, if not a bridge, for such travelers. This book was part of my journey, and it may become part of yours.

It was also written in part for my fellow religionists. When I was baptized as a Christian at the age of twenty-seven, I found that my search was far from over, indeed was only just beginning. But now it took a different form. I had found my way into a maze, but the maze itself remained to be traversed. I had found the home of truth, the place where everything I had ever loved in the world came to die and to be resurrected, but a long journey still lay before me — a journey into myself, a lifelong journey I would have to allow to transform me. I hope that some report of the maze and of my discoveries within it may be of service to others.

I want to thank Roy M. Carlisle of The Crossroad Publishing Company for his impetuous enthusiasm for this book, and his team for all their hard and careful work. Several friends read the text in draft at different stages and made helpful comments, including Dom Bernard Orchard, OSB, Fr. John

Saward, Aidan Nichols, OP, Scott Hahn, Phil Zaleski, David Meconi, SJ, Francesca Murphy, and Greg Glazov. Any mistakes of judgment, of course, remain my own. Leslie Pitcher kindly translated some medieval Latin for me. I am grateful to Fr. Ian Boyd, CSB, David L. Schindler, Robert Bolton, Michael Waldstein, and Adrian Walker for their friendship and encouragement. However, it was my wife, Léonie, who first revealed to me the mystery of the sacraments. If, as G. K. Chesterton tells us, "thanks is the highest form of thought," then I think of her most highly of all.

Discovering the Sacred Mysteries

There are mysteries buried in the text of Holy Scripture and in the Christian tradition, mysteries that still, after two thousand years of Christian commentary, remain unexplored and by many Christians even undiscovered. I am not speaking of such things as the so-called "bloodline of Jesus Christ," the stuff of popular fantasy, but of something much stranger, much harder to grasp. The Church struggled long and hard — is still struggling — against the pretensions of self-styled elites to possess a liberating "gnosis" or secret knowledge that has been concealed from the majority of Christians. But the heretical Gnostics were not entirely wrong: there is a *true* Christian gnosis, even if it is rather different from what they supposed. Saint Paul and the Alexandrian Church Fathers talk about it quite openly.

Knowing this, one of the greatest theologians of the twentieth century, Hans Urs von Balthasar, writes: "Even so truly a 'church of the people' as the Catholic Church does not abolish genuine esotericism. The secret path of the saints is never denied to one who is really willing to follow it. But who in the crowd troubles himself over such a path?"[1] Catholic philosopher Jean Borella speaks of the need to revive, among today's Christians, "a certain 'spirit of esoterism,' that is to say the sense of sacred mystery *and* of transcendent interiority. For 'the kingdom of heaven is like unto a treasure hidden in a field. Which a man having found, *hid it*, and for joy thereof goeth, and selleth all that he hath, and buyeth that field' (Matt. 13:14)."[2]

Scholarship alone is not sufficient to unlock these mysteries. They are accessible only to the explorer who is prepared to venture into the darkest landscapes of his own self, to find out *who he really is.* There is a modern academic tradition called historical-critical, which looks at biblical texts with a view to discovering who might have written them, and when and why. However valid and interesting this type of speculation may be, it is not the best way to understand the Christian mysteries. There can be no shortcut to a mystical understanding using techniques drawn from a secular discipline. The only road is a prayerful and intuitive exploration of Scripture in the light of tradition and of the actual practice of the Christian life.

The "secret" I am speaking of concerns the relationship between nature and grace; that is, between ourselves and God's action in our lives. How can we become free of all that binds us, all that constricts us? There is no one who does not yearn for freedom as he feels the bonds of age and infirmity, of spoiled relationships and wasted opportunities, of misunderstandings and wickedness, closing in around him. Time is running out, and have we yet discovered why we are here?

The Christian mysteries are mysteries of the Incarnation. They concern the ways in which we can become united with God through his Son, and so attain perfect freedom and joy. In the strictest sense they are identified with seven specific ritual actions of the Church we call "sacraments" (in Greek *ta mystēria*). Each of these actions reveals an aspect of Christ's saving and healing work. It is the meaning and connection of these mysteries within the context of the Christian Way that I hope will emerge from what follows. I am not offering a complete theology of the sacraments, which can be found in other books,[3] nor are my reflections put forward with any pretensions to ecclesial or academic authority; they are intended simply to encourage further exploration, just as they themselves arise from reflection upon the work of others in the midst of a busy life.

The emphasis I have placed upon numbers as an organizing principle is unfashionable, but neither unorthodox nor untraditional. According to the 1917 *Catholic Encyclopedia,* "although the Fathers repeatedly condemned the magical use of numbers which had descended from Babylonian sources to the Pythagoreans and Gnostics of their times, and although they denounced any system of their philosophy which rested upon an exclusively numerical basis, still they almost unanimously regarded the numbers of Holy Writ as full of mystical meaning, and they considered the interpretation of these mystical meanings as an important branch of exegesis." The *Encyclopedia* adds that "when the Church was forming her liturgy and when Christian teachers so readily saw mystical meanings underlying everything which had to do with numbers, it can hardly be doubted that a symbolical purpose must constantly have guided the repetition of acts and prayers in the ceremonial of the Holy Sacrifice and indeed in all public worship. Even in the formulae of the prayers themselves we meet unmistakable traces of this kind of symbolism."[4]

In fact, links and correspondences of the precisely the sort I am suggesting may be found in Saint Augustine, Saint Thomas (whose *Summa Theologiae* is partly organized around them), Hugh of Saint Victor, and Robert Grosseteste, right through to more modern and controversial figures such as Adrienne von Speyr (a mystic closely associated with von Balthasar) and the anonymous author of *Meditations on the Tarot* (who was actually a Catholic convert from anthroposophy named Valentin Tomberg). The latter's ideas were often unorthodox, but among the dubious teachings found in his book are scattered many profound insights. I have borrowed from these without feeling the need to follow him too precisely. In fact, when venturing into such areas it is necessary to exercise considerable discernment, for truth may be entangled with the most outrageous distortions, and the Gnostic temptation to consider oneself the member of an elite group of knowers is never far away. In this book I have therefore taken something of a risk by adopting an eclectic approach. I felt strengthened by a saying of Saint Ambrose and Saint Thomas Aquinas, *omne verum a quocumque dicatur a Spiritu Sancto est;* that is to say, any statement of truth is from the Holy Spirit, no matter who utters it. Nothing has been taken from the authors cited that I believe to be incompatible with the open and public teaching of the Church.

Notes

1. Von Balthasar, *The Glory of the Lord,* 1:34.
2. Borella, *Guénonian Esoterism and Christian Mystery,* 338.
3. Such as Haffner, *The Sacramental Mystery.*
4. Herbert Thurston, SJ, article on "Numbers," *Catholic Encyclopedia,* online at *www.newadvent.org/cathen/.* For more detail on this subject, see de Lubac, *Medieval Exegesis,* 84–89, and Hopper, *Medieval Number Symbolism.* It seems that any retrieval of tradition must take seriously the numerological aspects of Scripture. In both Hebrew and Greek, letters served as numbers. To ancient readers a given biblical text might also appear as mathematical code. If Scripture is divinely inspired, God's intentions should be discernible in mathematical as well as narrative structures. This was certainly the view of many Church Fathers.

ONE

The Mysteries of Christ

Sacraments are "powers that come forth" from the Body of Christ, which is ever-living and life-giving. They are actions of the Holy Spirit at work in his Body, the Church. They are "the masterworks of God" in the new and everlasting covenant.
— *Catechism of the Catholic Church,* para. 1116

It is remarkable how often we assume we know something simply because we have heard people talk about it. Years may go by, and then we suddenly realize that we never really understood what they were on about. That may happen at any level or stage of our lives. It happens to children, but it also happens to adults, no matter how educated or distinguished they may be. It happens to all of us, because it is part of the process by which we grow.

In the case of Christianity, there is no shame in admitting that we do not understand the least thing about it. It appears to us at times like an ideology, a system of thought and ideas that can be learnt and mastered like any other. I can inform myself about its tenets, I can decide between the various interpretations on offer, and I may or may not decide to accept it. But none of this is really Christianity: it is a human invention designed to take the place of Christianity. Christianity actually is a relationship not with an idea, but with a person — Jesus Christ. The reason we do not understand Christianity is that we understand neither Christ nor what it means to be in relationship with him.

The Lord

Jesus Christ is not simply one more person like any other, albeit one who rose from the dead and asks for our allegiance. Jesus is the "new Adam"; we are to become not merely friends but "members" of him. *Catholicism is therefore irreducibly mystical.* The Church is a mystical body, animated by a soul that comes from God and is God (the Holy Spirit). The institutional arrangements that we see when we look at the Church with our normal, earthly eyes are simply the skeleton that enables the body to walk around.[1] It takes eyes of faith to see the Church in the flesh, its bones clothed in the "flesh" of people like ourselves living — through Baptism — the extended life of Christ.

Who was Christ? He was more than a meteor dropped from heaven onto the earth. Or if in one sense he was a meteorite, he was one that contained eternity — the eternal life of God, which is the source of all love — and when he collided with the earth, he reshaped it around himself. Or he was a magnet that, once it was embedded in human history, drew history toward itself like so many iron filings, so that all mythologies, all intuitions, now point toward him and lead to him. But no metaphor or simile drawn from the inanimate can suffice. At its core the world is personal; it is a world of relationships that are deeper than what we call substance, and Jesus Christ was above all a *person*. It is through encountering him as a person, not as a merely physical body nor as a mere animal, that we are introduced to the true purpose and meaning of human life. In his every word and gesture while on earth, Eternity was expressing itself to man in the language of human existence, was inviting us into relationship with Itself, was showing us the way to become fully a person.

Jesus was born of Mary. This is another respect in which he was no meteorite, for he emerged from human history and a human bloodline. God is not only above us, in heaven, but *among* us, and it is from here that he emerges most surprisingly, almost invisibly, like a secret being breathed for the first time. He remains in this relationship with Mary, who is his mother forever. Thus when we look at Mary, we see the secret of Christ and the human face of the Church.

The Church

The Church begins with Mary, but it is the sacraments that make the Church. The sacraments are formal, symbolic actions by which Christ's saving and healing actions in the brief years of his earthly existence are extended through time into our own lives. In other words, by pouring his Spirit into the People of God, Christ's life, including his ministry among men and his sacrificial death, is shared out among all those who are baptized. Adrienne von Speyr writes of this most powerfully in the following passage from her little book on the sacraments: "His Body lives in them with the same vitality and certainty as the Son lived among men in his life on earth. Actually, he has only gone one step further: at that time he lived among us; now he lives in us. He has transposed the mystery of his Incarnation in to each individual believer. And he works from within each one, for into each he has placed the mirror of heaven by means of Communion. . . . A mirror of heaven sparkles at one point in the world, undiminished, uncompromising and endowed with the strength to transform man and his whole activity towards heaven."[2]

Tradition and the Church tell us that Christ "instituted" the sacraments. However, this needs to be understood correctly. While the Gospels do record several distinct moments of institution ("Go baptize," "Do this in memory of me"), these should not be taken as a series of more-or-less isolated and arbitrary acts of will. The sacraments are founded in our Lord's entire life, a life of supreme inner consistency, and the echoes of their institution can be found everywhere. The *Catechism* quotes with approval this statement of Pope Leo: "What our Redeemer did visibly has passed over into the sacraments."[3]

Since the twelfth century, the Catholic tradition has admitted precisely seven sacraments, three of initiation (Baptism, Confirmation, and Eucharist), two of healing (Reconciliation, also known as Confession, and the Anointing of the Sick), and two at the service of communion (Ordination and Marriage).[4] They were not all equally well delineated in the early Church, but the details of their development do not concern us here. All we need to understand is that the differentiation and consolidation of the seven sacraments is simply an unfolding of the life of Christ, which has seeded itself in the rich soil of the Church. That life, with all of Christ's human actions, was transposed into eternity at the Ascension, when Christ's resurrected body mysteriously went "up" into heaven. This reintegration with eternity made it possible for that life to be present to each of us here and now, at every moment in time. The sacraments thus become the means for drawing all men — and through them the entire cosmos of space and time — into an intimate personal relationship with the Father, into the everlasting liturgy of praise that is the business of heaven.

Christ appears after his resurrection to Mary Magdalen and is mistaken by her for a gardener (John 20:15). But Christ is indeed a gardener, as Adam was in the beginning, when he was

placed in the "paradise of pleasure," in Eden, to tend and culti-
vate it. Christ is the gardener of our souls, and of the Church.
He instituted the sacraments as a gardener institutes an apple
tree or a rose bush: by planting them. The seeds he planted
grew into the rituals that we know today. So our Lord did not
need to sit down with a group of canon lawyers to draft the
constitution of the Church. He simply lived and walked among
men and did the things that his Father sent him to do, such as
choosing the Apostles. These very actions form the constitution
of the Church.

The sacraments make the Church. So said Henri de Lubac, particularly of the Eucharist, but by extension it applies to all the
sacraments in some degree. It is the sacraments, not our good
deeds, and certainly not mere words (creeds and sermons), that
create the Church. Without them she would not exist at all.
The sacraments ensure that the Church is Christ's "body," not
a mere idea of him or a memory of him but his own life as a
human being, lived out in the men and women he came to save.

The Work

The implication of all this is more than we know how to grasp.
The sacraments are "actions of the Holy Spirit at work in his
Body, the Church."[5] This gift of grace through the action of the
Holy Spirit implies a participation in the very life of God —
the life of the Trinity. This defines the end or goal of the Christian life: holiness. Christianity is about transformation. "As fire
transforms into itself everything it touches, so the Holy Spirit
transforms into the divine life whatever is subjected to his
power."[6]

This goal of transformation, indeed of "deification" (*theosis*)
by the Holy Spirit, is not emphasized enough in Christian teaching. We tend to think that the Church wants us simply to behave

in a certain way (to "be good"), and so to be admitted to heaven. But the deeper understanding is right there in the *Catechism.*[7] It is that we are to become not merely "good," but "*gods.*"[8] We are to become something more than what we are now. "Beloved, we are God's children now; it does not yet appear what we shall be, but we know that when he appears we shall be like him, for we shall see him as he is" (1 John 3:2). Only like can see like, and theologians such as Saint Thomas tell us that in our final state we shall know God with God's own mind, as he knows himself.

Mystics speak of becoming "one" with God, of dying to ourselves or losing all sense of personal identity, as though the final goal of existence were nothing but self-destruction. That is to misunderstand the nature of the experience. Our personal identity is created by God; it does not matter whether we are conscious of ourselves or not, provided God is aware of us. The problem is that most of the time we act as though we were our own creators, desperately clinging to self-consciousness. This is the subtle form of something the Bible describes as idolatry — the worship of a false god. It places a golden image of ourselves, which is actually not only a false god but a false self, at the center of our lives.

In Christ, in the sacramental life of the Church, I become my true self, which is a unity — a united, integrated entity. My *false self* is far from united; it is multitudinous, legion, and all the parts are at war with one another. In fact, little false selves are being created in me all the time, as my desires pull me in this direction or that. I can observe the budding of a false self taking place whenever I sin against my conscience, doing something that part of me wants to do but the rest of me knows is wrong. My imagination latches on to this selfish act and uses it to weave an image of myself, investing much of my soul's energy into the image. If contrition and absolution do not dissolve the false self, the sin will grow within me and become a distinct force, enslaving my personality. Vivifying contact with the living waters of Baptism and Reconciliation can dissolve that hard knot in my soul.

Thus the life of man and the life of God have been inescapably entangled together ever since the Incarnation. Von Balthasar speaks of God's self-revelation as taking place in the loving sacrifice of his life on the Cross: "In this final intensification not only are we shown that God is love; at the same time it becomes manifest that, in the revelation of his love in flesh and blood, and in the sacrifice of these for the life of the world, God has committed himself unsurpassably and beyond all return. Whoever has been able to read the image of the Son who bled to death on the Cross will not then be really 'surprised' by the prolongation of this commitment in the Eucharist. The Eucharist will be regarded by such a person only as a dimension emerging from that first commitment. Nor, in this context, can the resurrection of the flesh and the eternal Marriage-feast of the Lamb and his Bride give cause for wonder: all of it is already included in the self-commitment of God, who with divine freedom, but also with divine consistency, *has fashioned for himself in his creation a body through which to reveal his glory.*" [9]

Symbolic Realism

In order to understand the sacraments we have to have an understanding of symbolism and its cosmic importance. For the sacraments are *rituals*, which means they are symbolic actions, and they make use of objects or elements such as water and oil that themselves are rich in symbolic properties and associations.

Symbolism is the primary language in which God addresses us. "Everything in nature is a symbol and everything that happens is a parable." [10] The symbolic is the basis of the sacramental order. When God takes a symbolic or ritual form and fills it with his own presence, the symbol then becomes an extension of his Incarnation as a man among men. For Christians it follows that *in no other way* than by training our symbolic consciousness can the basis be established for a continued, living interest in the truths of faith and the possibility of spiritual progress.

The loss of symbolic consciousness in modern times is closely linked to the collapse of effective catechesis in homes, parishes, and schools. We all have an instinctive appreciation of symbols, at least as children, but the development of full-fledged rationalism in the eighteenth and nineteenth centuries meant that (for adults) symbolism was increasingly disparaged, as though it were nothing but the subjective projection of our own concerns on to an alien cosmos. According to the modern rationalist, patterns in nature arise by chance through a process of evolution; they cannot actually "mean" anything. For a thing to "mean" something there must be a degree of intention involved. I may use water in a story with the intention of saying something about the idea of purity, for example, but the meaning is subjective because I have imposed it myself. By contrast, the Christian tradition (and of course every religious tradition the world over) claims that the world of nature is not produced by chance alone. That implies the possibility of *objective* meaning, objective symbolism. For example, we might say that God, the power or reality who is behind the universe as a whole, creates or intends the element Water partly as a way of expressing the quality of purity that exists in himself.

If things are indeed created, then the true "meaning" of anything is what God intends by it. What philosophers in the tradition of Saint Thomas call its "act of existence" is an act of *meaning something;* that is, creation is an intentional act on the part of the Creator. It follows that the natural world is a world of objective symbols. There is nothing that is not a "word." Each level of reality corresponds with the others analogically. Each is more in "act" (as the scholastics would say) than the one below it, and so "in-forms" it. Since everything in the visible world is the manifestation in matter of a particular Form, each and every created thing is a symbol of its own interior essence, and the world is a radiant book of symbols to be read with eyes that are sensitive to spiritual light. Symbols are not mere signs pointing to something distant and removed, but bridges connecting and joining one thing to another, making something present that would otherwise be absent.[11]

The Victorian poet Coventry Patmore speaks of the symbolic and more or less enigmatic language employed by the Church and the authors of Scripture.[12] This compels, he says, "a state of active co-operation, a voluntary excitement of the mind, greatly more favourable to the abiding effect of moral truths and impressions than is the state of merely passive attention. This mode of reception includes the act of reflection, without which no knowledge ever becomes our own." It is also "the very method of Nature, whose book, from beginning to end, is nothing but a series of symbols, enigmas, parables, and rites, only to be interpreted by the 'discerning intellect of man,' actively and laboriously employed."

Furthermore, Patmore writes that it "would be of great use to many if the meaning of a few of the principal of the symbolic words common to all the great religions were made a part of religious instruction; though it is wonderful how, by a sort of instinct, some of these keys are discerned and read by the simplest and least instructed who, among their low surroundings, lead pure and meditative lives." For, as he says, "The names of the four chief points of the compass, water, fire, cloud, thunder, lightning, nation, generation, father, mother, son, daughter, rich, poor, tree, stone, fish, mountains, bird, rod, flower, leaf, etc., etc., have fixed significances without the knowledge of which thousands of passages of Scripture, even those not involving any enigmatic meaning, cannot be understood."

He goes on to distinguish *objective* imagery, which expresses realities by means of things having some resemblance to them, from *phonetic* imagery, which uses sounds that possess a subtle correspondence to things. These lie at the origin of written and spoken language respectively, and by their combination give rise to poetry (which he calls "the only *real* speech" of all nations and times). He speaks also of *parabolic* meanings, exemplified in the use or enactment of teaching parables that carry multiple, perhaps inexhaustible, layers of meaning to those who have ears to hear. Thus, he warns, "The rites, customs, architecture, ornaments, and vestures of the Church are stores of more or less enigmatic teaching, and not one can be destroyed or altered without the risk of some unknown loss." (In this light, of course, the wholesale iconoclasm and philistinism of liturgical and architectural "experts" in the late twentieth century appear even more disastrous.)

It is poets like Patmore who have kept alive this sense of the true origins and symbolic power of words and images. One might speak in this connection of Gerard Manley Hopkins and David Jones, of Paul Claudel and Charles Péguy.

But sacrament goes further than symbolism. Famously, when a guest at a dinner party she was attending said that the Eucharist was a "symbol of Christ," the American Catholic writer Flannery O'Connor burst out, "Well, if it's only a symbol, to hell with it!" Catholics believe that the Eucharist is much more than a symbol. The symbolic properties of bread and wine, heightened as they are by the ritual in which they are embedded, are merely the natural contribution to a supernatural action. In more measured tones, von Balthasar also explains that more than symbolism is involved when he writes: "No matter how much dynamic movement the form of revelation may be thought to contain, this form is more than a Platonic economy of symbolic signs which point beyond themselves to a spiritual reality — even if the dynamism of this expressive form leads us down into the depths of the Passion, the Death and Hades itself, and then up to the heights of an Ascension which withdraws the sensory image from our senses for our greater good."[13]

A Platonic interpretation of Catholicism would insist that the rituals and particularly the sacraments are divinely inspired symbols that raise the mind above the things of the flesh to a spiritual realm that is more real than they are. Von Balthasar is saying that you can take this kind of interpretation quite a long way — even far enough to give a good account of the descent into hell and the ascension to heaven — but that it misses something vital. It captures the ascent of the mind to God, but it misses the descent of God to earth.

When God's own Word, the Word that was with God and is God (according to the prologue of John's Gospel), comes to be uttered as the ultimate fulfillment of the whole process of God's self-communication, it employs the symbolic properties of creation but raises them to a new level — a new level of meaning, but also of existence.

The Incarnation — by which we signify the "hypostatic union" (union in a person) of a human and a divine nature — is the archetype, if you like, of what goes on in every natural symbol. Every symbol mediates between the divine and the human realm. In its earthly nature a symbol partakes of the human, but its *form* reveals an interior light that shines from heaven. This is similar to the relationship we find in the God-Man, between his human nature and his divinity, although in this case the union is ineffably superior, being that of a person (*hypostasis*), which is the highest and most central thing in the world, all else being peripheral and fragmentary in relation to it.

Everything the Son does on earth is an act of giving — for God is love, which means self-gift. Everything he does is an act of communication — for communication is a giving of oneself, and love (or self-giving) is the only way one person may be known by another. All natural symbols, or all the naturally symbolic properties of the cosmos into which the Son is plunged, are subsumed within this act of giving and of communication. This is how bread and wine, water and oil, the laying on of hands and the breathing of the Spirit, come to be more than just symbols of heavenly things. They are assumed into the action of the Incarnation, enfolded within the hypostatic union. What Jesus Christ does with his hands is not simply symbolic of what God always does in heaven: it is what God is doing, right now, right here on earth.

The sacraments are symbols, but they are also more than symbols. They occupy a level of reality between the naturally symbolic cosmos and the man who is God. They extend the actions he performed on earth. In that sense they are parts of his "mystical" body, and in fact they generate that body in something of the way a seed generates a plant or an animal. For the Church is a supernatural organism that grows and develops over time, just as we do.

The Sevenfold Way in Scripture

In the last century the French Jesuit Henri de Lubac, among others, helped to recover for us the importance of the *spiritual* exegesis (interpretation) of the Bible in the light of tradition.[14] The danger of falling into subjectivism and simply "discovering" in Scripture whatever one wants to find there, which is the normal accusation made against such interpretation, is ever present. For de Lubac, and the Church Fathers whose method he helped to retrieve, the best control on the wilder kind of individual speculation was the embeddedness of the text within the Church, whose authority is final, and with whose official interpretations any other meaning must be both consistent and coherent.[15]

That said, the horizon of interpretation of Scripture, for de Lubac, was wide indeed. In the following passage from his magisterial survey of medieval exegesis he weaves together citations from various Church Fathers to express Scripture's limitless potentiality: "Scripture is like the world: 'undecipherable in its fullness and in the multiplicity of its meanings.' A deep forest, with innumerable branches, 'an infinite forest of meanings': the more involved one gets in it, the more one discovers that it is impossible to explore it right to the end. It is a table arranged by Wisdom, laden with food, where the unfathomable divinity of the Savior is itself offered as nourishment to all. Treasure of the Holy Spirit, whose riches are as infinite as himself. True labyrinth. Deep heavens, unfathomable abyss. Vast sea, where there is endless voyaging 'with all sails set.' Ocean of mystery."[16]

Few people in modern times have better demonstrated the limitless potentiality of Scripture than Adrienne von Speyr, the Swiss mystic who along with de Lubac has already found her way into these pages. With Hans Urs von Balthasar she cofounded the Community of Saint John in Switzerland. I find it hard not to be moved by her spiritual commentaries, nor to feel that our understanding of Revelation has been expanded by them. *The Cross: Word and Sacrament* focuses on Jesus's seven last words from the Cross, which she says constitute "an authentic self-interpretation of the sufferings of redemption, a direct translation of the Passion into words." They are Jesus's "legacy," words of power forged in the heat of the Passion, words by which he creates the Church. And the Church, in von Speyr's

vision of things, is no mere institution: the Church is the extension of the Incarnation, implicit in every action of the Redeemer,
born from the womb of the Cross.

Von Speyr goes further. "If the Lord's words are all of a
piece with his life, and if he surrenders his life on the Cross
for his Church, it follows that the Lord's words from the Cross
are closely knit to, parallel to, the sacraments, those vessels of
the life of divine grace which overflows from the Cross to the
Church." Think of it this way: if Jesus is God, then everything
he does or says is a revelation. Nothing happens by chance.
If he became man in order to save us from death by dying
on the Cross, then everything that happens during his Passion
in particular is weighted with a special significance for us —
which the Church acknowledges by recapitulating those events
in the Liturgy, echoing a similar emphasis within Holy Scripture
(and indeed Scripture and Liturgy can hardly be separated).
And our Lord's last moments as he hangs upon the Cross are
the most precious of all, the most concentrated. Scripture and
tradition tell us of precisely seven utterances from the Cross,
which reveal a deep structure within the life of the Church.
Adrienne[17] therefore links each of the Last Words to one of the
sacraments.

She begins with the sacrament of Reconciliation (which she
normally refers to as Confession): *"Father, forgive them for they
know not what they do."* She writes: "This first of the Lord's words
contains his whole life's purpose. He hangs on the Cross in
order to achieve for sinners their forgiveness before God." This
is "not the private plea of a goodhearted man who for some
reason or other is being tortured and utters a prayer for his
tormentors," it is rather "the request of the world's Redeemer
in the exercise of his redeeming office." He does not aim simply
(as some forms of Protestantism would imply) to "cover over"
the sins that have placed him on the Cross, which the different

stages of the Passion reveal in all their ghastly detail; for "it is not enough for the Father to see his suffering, to behold this crushing transfer of responsibility from men to him; he wants the Father to accept men as being guiltless, and this innocence will only be achieved by the Cross being prolonged and taking shape in the Church's practice of Confession, whereby men can have their share of sanctifying grace."

In order actually to transform men by grace from being sinners to being saints, Christ must bring them into his life so the Father will see them in him, and he does this by means of the Church's sacraments. Thus in each confession, a Christian is participating in the Son's act of self-sacrifice on the Cross, viewing this as a confession, an exposure to the Father's gaze, of the world's sin. And, looking at the same thing from the other side, the Son is present at every Christian's confession, pleading for them to the Father, "personally supplying what is just, requisite, necessary and true, and contributing what is lacking." They "know not what they do"; until, that is, they come to the Cross and see what they have done. In seeing it, they are able to reject their sin as no longer belonging to them, and be absolved, the Cross becoming their doorway into eternal life.[18]

The second sacrament listed by Adrienne von Speyr is Anointing (which used to be called Extreme Unction), which is linked to the Word: *Today you will be with me in Paradise.* This is addressed to the good thief, the one who, of the two crucified with him, does not curse but acknowledges his own guilt and has faith in the Lord ("Remember me when you come into your kingdom"). Adrienne calls this sacrament, the sacrament of approaching death, a "second Baptism," adding that it occupies "precisely the place which Baptism could have occupied if man had remained in the state of innocence." The thief is as much our representative as the disciple John, who stands at the foot of the Cross.

The third sacrament is Marriage, which Adrienne links to the words, *"Woman, behold your son. Son, behold your mother."* In giving John to Mary and Mary to John, in making them mother and child to each other by identifying himself with the "disciple he loved," Jesus reveals his Passion as akin to the consummation of a marriage, the marriage of his divine and human natures, or of heaven and earth. The fruit of this includes all the Christians who, like John, take Mary as their spiritual mother and "make a place for her" in their homes. "The blessing from the Cross institutes the nuptial blessing," Adrienne writes, deliberately blurring the distinction between the two relationships, spousal and filial. The spiritual bond here transcends the biological: John is not Mary's biological offspring, and if she is the archetypal woman (the term Jesus uses to address her) then John stands here as the archetypal man, in the place of a virginal spouse as well as a spiritual son. Perhaps in relation to Woman every man, even a husband, is in some sense a child.

The fourth sacrament in Adrienne's list is Ordination. *"My God, my God, why have you forsaken me?"* All that remains to Jesus is his mission, his priestly service, projected now into utter darkness. But that mission serves to build a road over the void. "The Son's cry is a prophecy, an anticipation, bearing *in advance* all that will happen to those who are his, who really belong to him, taking seriously the risk of discipleship — all those who were willing to dedicate themselves and now find themselves faced with the void, because they chose the void out of love for mankind; because they did not want human security and company but the naked will of God. And this has led them where they did not wish to go." (Though Adrienne does not say so, Psalm 22 from which Jesus takes these words, and which is therefore now the Psalm of priesthood, ends on a note of hope rather than despair.)

The fifth sacrament is Eucharist, which she links to the words *"I thirst."* A phrase that has been attributed both to Saint Augustine and to Saint Gregory is sometimes embroidered on the cloth that covers the altar in more traditional Catholic churches: *sitit sitiri* — "He thirsts to be thirsted for." This neatly captures the deep paradox of the Lord's eucharistic presence. He must thirst in order to be able to give "living water" to others. They must thirst for him, and he must feel that thirst on their behalf; indeed, he gives it to them. "Because he emptied himself until his whole self was nothing but a burning void," Adrienne says, "we possess him in us as Eucharist."

The sixth sacrament is Baptism, linked to the words, *"It is accomplished."* We are baptized, Saint Paul tells us, into the death of Christ. His earthly end is the beginning of our eternal life. In the sacrament of Baptism the founding of the Church is "accomplished." It is finished, the sacrifice is completed: he has given all that he has.

And the seventh sacrament is closely associated with the sixth — it is Confirmation. *"Father, into your hands I commend my Spirit."* Having given all that he has to give to man, the gift is now entrusted to the Father. The Holy Spirit who accompanied the Son is sent back to the Father in order to descend at the right time on Pentecost, bestowing or confirming spiritual gifts — themselves sevenfold, corresponding again to the sacraments. As Adrienne puts it: "As it grows dark around the Cross, the Spirit ascends once more to the Father's brightness, soon to return to the world's darkness bearing the fiery flames of eternal life. Faith will recognize him by his glory as the Spirit of the Three-in-One."

I find Adrienne von Speyr's intuitions compelling, and my hypothesis in this book is merely a rather audacious extension of hers. I try to show that each of the sacraments can be linked not only to the Last Words, but to other sevenfold mysteries such as the seven archetypal miracles wrought in the Gospel of John, the seven "I am" sayings in the same Gospel, the seven great petitions in the Lord's Prayer sometimes called the Our Father, and the seven days of creation narrated in the book of Genesis.[19]

Notes

1. Von Balthasar, in *The Glory of the Lord* (559), resists any description of the "institution" as a kind of "skeleton, outside destiny and time." But I am not intending here to separate the institutional elements from the personal. The human skeleton is a part of the person.

2. Von Speyr, *The Gates of Eternal Life*, 52–53.

3. *Catechism of the Catholic Church*, para. 1115.

4. In other words, three that are foundational for our membership of the Church, two that serve the individual soul, and two that exist for the sake of the community. See *Catechism of the Catholic Church*, paras. 1210 to 1666. This section of the *Catechism* lays out the Church's teaching on the sacraments in detail.

5. *Catechism*, para. 1116.

6. *Catechism*, para. 1127; cf. paras. 1113 to 1658.

7. For example, the *Catechism* paras. 1692 and 1721 quotes Saint Peter to the effect that we are to become "partakers of the divine nature" (1 Pet. 1:4). See also paras. 1997, 1998 about the way grace comes through the sacraments to make this possible.

8. And who is truly good but God himself? Cf. Matt. 19:17. But our Lord also says, quoting Scripture, "You are gods" (John 10:34). C. S. Lewis, in a famous sermon called "The Weight of Glory," puts it beautifully: "It is a serious thing to live in a society of possible gods and goddesses, to remember that the dullest and most uninteresting person you talk to may one day be a creature which, if you saw it now, you would be strongly tempted to worship."

9. Von Balthasar, *The Glory of the Lord*, 1:440–41. My emphasis.

10. Claudel, *The Essence of the Bible*, 13.

11. Philosophically speaking, "symbolic realism" is a type of realism, opposed therefore to nominalism, but it goes further than merely claiming that universals are real: it insists that the very existence of particulars is a symbolic act, that is, an intentional act on the part of God who thereby expresses himself in the creature. Cf. Borella, *The Secret of the Christian Way*.

12. Patmore, *Religio Poetae Etc.*, ch. III.

13. Ibid., 440.

14. Tradition had defined four distinct "senses," levels or types of inter-pretation of Scripture: the literal (historical) and tropological (moral) on the one hand, and the two mystical senses, the allegorical (pertaining to salvation history) and anagogical (pertaining to the divine life), on the other. See Wood, *Spiritual Exegesis and the Church in the Theology of Henri de Lubac.* Variants on this tradition preferred three senses (for body, soul, and spirit) or else seven, as suggested by the Book of Revelation with its "seven seals" (Rev. 5:1) and "seven spirits of God" (Rev. 4:5; 5:6). See de Lubac, *Medieval Exegesis,* 84–89.

15. How one attains a greater freedom of thought through submission to the teaching authority of the Church is a matter I will not discuss in detail here, though it has something to do with the fact that "limits" are actually essential to the exercise of freedom. G. K. Chesterton pointed out that it is the physical limitations of canvas and paint which give the artist his freedom to create a portrait, and the rules of chess that constitute the game. Without the limitations there would be no freedom. In the case of thinking, we all base our arguments on certain assumptions. Thought has to start somewhere. Every rocket needs a launch pad. Human beings, and not just religious believers, are inevitably "dogmatic"; the challenge for us is to choose the right set of dogmas — dogmas that correspond to the nature of reality itself.

16. De Lubac, *Medieval Exegesis,* 75.

17. Here I will let myself slip into referring to her by her first name, which is not uncommon in the literature, and which somehow feels more appropriate in these spiritual meditations than it might in some academic treatise.

18. Adrienne von Speyr devoted a major work to the sacrament of *Confession,* which is listed in the bibliography.

19. The book of Genesis, of course, is the odd one out in this series, being a part of the Old Testament. However, it seems extremely likely that the Gospel writers, especially John, had the Jewish Scriptures and particularly Genesis in mind as they composed their own writings (though naturally they would not have had a developed theology of the seven sacraments). The Fourth Gospel opens with an account, essentially, of the creation of the world in the Word, and goes on to describe its re-creation in Christ, the Word Incarnate. The sacraments are the instruments of this re-creation; this is the basis for thinking that they may correspond to the pattern of the first creation.

T W O

A Cosmic Liturgy

*This action of God, which takes place through human speech, is
the real "action" for which all of creation is in expectation. The
elements of the earth are transubstantiated, pulled, so to speak,
from their creaturely anchorage, grasped at the deepest ground of
their being, and changed into the Body and Blood of the Lord. The
New Heaven and New Earth are anticipated. The real "action" in
the liturgy in which we are all supposed to participate is the action
of God himself.*   — Joseph Ratzinger[1]

Since in this book we are reflecting on the Church's inner structure or "DNA" — her sacramental structure — we must pay
some attention specifically to the central point or axis of that
structure, namely the Eucharist. This word is used to refer to
the sacred elements after the consecration has turned the bread
and wine into a different "substance," namely Christ. But what
Catholics call transubstantiation only takes place within an extended ritual action called the Mass, which is also referred to
as Eucharist. The Orthodox simply call it the Divine Liturgy.

The Eucharist is a peculiarly dynamic sacrament. It is designed to look like a meal of a rather formal or stylized kind,
but the essence of what takes place is both a banquet and a sacrifice. This connects it directly with the sacrament of Ordination
(priesthood), for a priest traditionally performs a sacrifice on

behalf of the people. A man is consecrated as a priest in the context of a Mass and primarily to celebrate Mass — the hearing of confessions and the preaching of the Gospel are intrinsically related to the performance of the sacrifice.

But what is a sacrifice? Why is it necessary? Rather than try to summarize the long history of ritual sacrifice in humanity's various religions, I want to relate it straightaway to the most characteristic doctrines of Christianity, namely the Incarnation and the Trinity, so we can see what is going on in the Eucharist, and what makes this a uniquely Christian sacrifice.

We often slip into thinking that God is like us. The reality is rather that *we are like him.* The analogy works in only one direction. But one of the moments when that resemblance is greatest is during the celebration of the Mass. That sacramental action is an echo or symbol of a sacrifice that is eternally taking place in God. But the heavenly sacrifice is not something that is merely being done by God; it *is* God. It is not done by the Holy Trinity; it *is* the Holy Trinity. The Father is always pouring himself out for the Son, the Son is eternally offering himself to the Father, and the Holy Spirit is the divine nature given and received — the "gift" that passes eternally between them. The link or connection between this heavenly Trinity (this ecstatic and eternal act of love that is God) and our earthly Mass is, of course, the Incarnation. Here is a man who is also God, whose sacrificial act as a man is also the sacrificial act of God.

At the heart of the Mass is a self-sacrificial act that takes place both in heaven and on the Cross. The Mass is not an imitation of what happens in heaven between the Father and the Son, nor a repetition of Christ's sacrifice on Calvary, but a sacrament, which is to say that it makes both those events "present" for us, wherever and whenever it is celebrated. Those who attend the Mass are standing with Mary and John at the foot of the Cross (as they are so often shown standing, in the images that stand in our churches behind or above the altar). And those who receive Communion, taking the transformed elements of bread and wine, which have now become the body and blood of Christ, into their own bodies, have an even more intimate relationship with this act.

It is sometimes said that the Mass is like a time machine because it places us at the foot of the Cross. But it first takes us to a point shortly *before* Christ's sacrificial death: it takes us to the Last Supper. For the Mass begins with a Liturgy of the Word which presents the congregation with selected passages of sacred Scripture, followed by a homily. Then, after prayer, and after solemnly reaffirming the Church's faith, the priest and people together make an offering of bread and wine in remembrance (the Greek word, *anamnesis*, implies something stronger than mere commemoration) of that Supper that the Lord took with his disciples shortly before his death.

As Romano Guardini once wrote: "It is very important to experience the Passover of the sacred moment emerging from eternity. It catches us up into itself, and while it lasts we are different from what we are at all other times. Then it dismisses us, and we fall back into the transitoriness of day-to-day existence. But if we have vitally participated in it, we take with us the seed of that holy eternity which comes from the Resurrection, and our life in the transitory world is changed."[2]

At the center of the Mass is a human offering that becomes a divine offering. What is raised up to the Father from the altar is the body and blood, the soul and divinity of his Son. In other words, the miracle of the Mass enables us to give the Father what he has given us to give. This represents the consummation of the spiritual life. Another quotation may help us glimpse the depths of what is being said here. Edith Stein (Saint Teresa Benedicta) was a Carmelite of Jewish origin who was killed by the Nazis. In her book *The Science of the Cross,* commenting on the *Living Flame* of her great teacher, Saint John of the Cross, she writes: "In the bridal surrender not only is one's own will subordinated and conformed with the divine one, but the divine surrender is also received. For this reason, in surrendering one's own person, one takes possession of God in a way so daring that it surpasses all human understanding. John of the Cross gives clear expression to this when he says that the soul can now give God *more* than she is herself: she gives to God, God himself in God.... It is a union of persons that does not end their independence, but rather has it as a prerequisite, an interpenetration that is surpassed only by the circumincession of the divine persons upon which it is modeled."[3]

The following briefly presents what actually happens in the Mass, dividing the action into seven main sections: (1) the Introductory Rite, (2) the Penitential Rite, (3) the Liturgy of the Word (which runs from the Gloria to the Gospel), (4) the Offertory, (5) the Consecration, (6) Holy Communion, and (7) the Rite of Dismissal. Each of these parts echoes one of the sacraments, in the following order: (1) Baptism, (2) Reconciliation, (3) Confirmation, (4) Ordination, (5) Eucharist, (6) Marriage, and (7) Anointing.[4] Each part of the Mass is examined in turn, bearing this association with the sacraments in mind.

1. **Introductory Rite (Baptism).** This sacred rite always begins with the sign of the Cross, which is also the symbol of the holy Trinity, in whose name every Christian is baptized. The gesture serves as a symbolic gateway into sacred space and sacred time. I always feel a strange reluctance to look at my watch during the Mass, once the ritual has begun. To enter into the spirit of the celebration is to be partially removed from secular time and implanted within the world of the angels.[5] We cannot help feeling

this, though we may not be able to put it into words. For a Catholic church to have a clock on the wall in some prominent place would seem to me like a desecration.

2. **Penitential Rite (Reconciliation).** This rite constitutes a kind of "clearing of the decks," spiritually speaking. It is not a substitute for sacramental confession, which it presupposes, but a communal act of repentance for the minor sins committed since sacramental absolution was last received in private. This is no encouragement to wallow in guilt, but a realistic and formal way of reorienting ourselves toward God in order to be able to receive what he wishes to give us. The invocation, "Lord have mercy, Christ have mercy, Lord have mercy," is directed to God as Trinity.

3. **Liturgy of the Word (Confirmation).** Here God gives us his Word. The readings from Scripture, both Old and New Testament, are to be *heard liturgically;* that is, they are not merely Bible stories that may be either quite familiar or quite obscure, either as literature or as history, rather they are the proclamation of God's revelation to us in the present moment. Perhaps they will sound to us as though we had never heard them before, since the moment in which we hear them is new. There is a sacramental virtue in the words that corresponds to Pentecost and thus to the sacrament of Confirmation. Provided that we manage to open our ears and hearts to them, such words can become like seeds falling onto fertile ground, bearing the Holy Spirit's life-force within them. It is part of the priest's work to reflect on the readings in his homily (sermon) in order to help them have this effect. He is, thus, planting seeds in the souls of his congregation. This part of the Mass is concluded with a recitation of the Creed, which

sums up the whole of Revelation in an inspired form, uniting the fragments of the Bible just read with the great ocean of truth.

4. **Offertory (Eucharist).** Now we move from the Liturgy of the Word to the heart of the Mass. The congregation offers bread and wine prepared on their behalf for the priest to consecrate. A collection plate may be passed around. These tokens represent human work and lives, as well as the whole created world that has entered into the making of these substances — through the soil, the plants, the farm animals who played their part, indeed even the lowly earthworm that tilled the soil, the wind and rain and sunshine. The priest takes these gifts and offers them to God, for God to accept and transform them into an even greater offering, the Eucharist itself. The whole world — and not just the human world — is involved in the liturgy, and all that has been offered here will be raised up on the last day as part of a resurrection earth.

5. **Consecration (Ordination).** This act, bound up as it is with the invocation of the Holy Spirit (*epiclesis*) surrounding it, is the solemn ritual whereby the Mass becomes an extension of the Last Supper. But the Last Supper was the anticipation of the Passion or death of our Lord on the Cross, which in turn was the earthly image and incarnation of the eternal sacrifice in heaven. This is the moment the sacrament of Ordination receives its most perfect expression. The priest raises up all our earthly giving, every aspect of our lives that has not been deliberately held back or turned away from God's face, to become a part of the self-giving of the Son to the Father, in heaven as it is on earth. In the most ancient prayers (the so-called Roman

Canon), reference is made to an angel that bears the sacrifice between the earthly and heavenly altars. The identity of the angel is unknown, but perhaps it is the angel of the priest.

6. **Holy Communion (Marriage).** We do not have to receive the consecrated body and blood of our Lord at every Mass, but the priest does, and most people also want to. Why, since the great sacrifice has already been accomplished at the altar of God? You might as well ask why a couple having made their vows of Marriage should not want to postpone the honeymoon. United with Christ in the sacrifice that has made us one flesh, that interior union is consummated with the mingling of our bodies, a symbolic giving and receiving that enables a new spiritual grace to come into our lives, making them more spiritually fruitful.

7. **Rite of Dismissal (Anointing).** Though brief, the dismissal (*Ite missa est*) brings the whole liturgy together in a single act of blessing and sending (*missio*). We are sent out into the world to complete the action of the Mass in our own lives: at home, at work, at school. If we have participated effectively in the Mass, we will have been healed of our sins and prepared even for death, as we are in the sacrament of Anointing. We go out from the sacred precinct marked, finally, with the sign of the Trinity.

We can see even from this brief account that the Church's Divine Liturgy is cosmic, in that it implicates and involves in some way the whole of creation. Marked throughout by the sign of three (the Trinity), its rich sevenfold structure is the particular concern of this book.

Transubstantiation

The Catholic Church teaches that the bread and wine used in the Catholic Mass change when they are consecrated by an ordained priest.[6] Their "substances" are converted into those of Christ's body and blood. This change, known as "transubstantiation," is not the kind that shows up in a microscope, and in fact is not accessible to the physical senses at all. The appearances (sometimes called, confusingly, the "accidents")[7] of the bread and wine remain as they were. This means, among other things, that a priest who is allergic to gluten will still be allergic to the Host after it is consecrated. The Orthodox Church also believes in the real presence of Christ in the sacrament, and at least one important Orthodox account from the fourteenth century (that of Nicholas Cabasilas) echoes quite closely the Latin teaching on the change that takes place. The Orthodox, however, tend to view the more important moment in the Divine Liturgy as the *epiclesis* or invocation of the Holy Spirit rather than the words of consecration, and although they may sometimes reserve the blessed sacrament in the sanctuary, they do not have a distinct service of adoration in the way the Catholic Church does.[8] (As we shall see, the really important thing is the *intention* which lies behind and is expressed by the Liturgy as a whole, as well as by the precise words of consecration whose meaning can only be understood in that context. The divine power of the Holy Spirit brings about the change in accordance with that intention.)

The meaning of the real presence is hard for modern people to grasp. Materialists grow up thinking that the substance of anything is the same as its physical composition: the substance of a pot is clay, and the substance of a ring is the gold it is made from. A physical material may be analyzed further into molecules and atoms, and if necessary those atoms may be further subdivided, and so on. On these assumptions, of course, little sense can be made of the Catholic or Orthodox teaching. Traditional metaphysics, on the other hand, identifies a substance not as what a thing is *made up of*, but what we grasp when we perceive it as a thing in the first place. Take a sugar cube. The cubeness of it is a form that, while it can be described, cannot be broken down in the way the sugar can be fragmented into crystals and then molecules. The sweetness of it is also a form or quality that is not reducible to anything else. These qualities inhabit the world of our perception but somehow transcend it. Each quality reveals some aspect of being, some portion of what it is *to be*. We are used to calling such qualities subjective, assuming that they are the effects on our individual nervous systems of the reality, namely molecules and patterns of energy. But in fact a thing is simply a synthesis of these qualities, grasped by us as actually existing. By contrast the molecular components of a thing (the basis of substance in the modern sense) are merely smaller things of roughly the same sort. The metaphysical *form* of the thing — that which makes it what it is — disappears from view as soon as we break it down into these components.

The Christian who accepts transubstantiation is obliged to distinguish a thing's physical makeup from the substance that constitutes its true reality. The word *substance* implies that this stands *sub-*, or under, the thing, but we could equally think of it as lying metaphorically above or within it. The Church does not specify the correct philosophical account of such a distinction. Some theologians believe that the most promising direction to look is in terms of some kind of Trinitarian account of existence that goes further, and is more dynamic, than the categories of Greek or even much Thomistic thought. Joseph Ratzinger (Pope Benedict XVI) once went so far as to write that Trinitarian theology conceals "a revolution in man's view of the world; the undivided sway of thinking in terms of substance is ended; relation is discovered as an equally valid primordial mode of reality."[9] To be a created substance is not to exist in oneself, but to exist within the Trinity, which is to say in and between the divine persons as a (limited) expression of their infinite self-giving to one another. This is to exist as an *act* rather than a *thing.*

This view is perfectly traditional, yet many people will find it changes their appreciation of what it is to exist, to be a substance. It is dynamic in the sense that it also implies things around us are not fully real *yet:* they exist, but they are not complete or finished — "perfected." They are in process, *in via,* on their way to being fully themselves. They have their end or goal in the life of the Trinity. They become real only by way of the Son's incarnation, death, resurrection, and ascension. Consciously or unconsciously it is through the Church (i.e., through the sacraments) that things become what they were meant to be eternally in God, by being received, by being given, by being transformed.

What a thing *is,* therefore, is not simply what God knows (or what we know when we grasp it). That would be too "static." As discussed in the earlier section on symbolic realism, an act of knowing is not separable from an act of willing: that which is known is always God's intention to express a particular aspect of the divine nature. Self-expression is a form of self-gift. The substances of bread and wine are transformed in the Mass because God is now giving not merely a particular aspect of his nature in these substances, but his very Self. He does this simply by willing it, and the intention to do so is made present by the priest's words spoken in the person of Christ and on his authority.[10]

But nothing *appears* to change. In a similar way, when a person is baptized, nothing *appears* to change. Regrettably enough, when one is received into the Church, one's friends do not necessarily notice a dramatic transformation in one's behavior. Yet in both these cases, with Baptism and Confirmation, a real (ontological) change does take place. Our reception of Christ in the Eucharist is meant to unite us with him and ultimately transform us into him. Saint Augustine, for example, tells us that the food we receive at the eucharistic table consumes us into itself, rather than the other way around. "When baptized, you were moistened into dough. On receiving the fire of the Holy Spirit, you were baked. Be what you see; receive what you are."[11]

The modern Orthodox writer Olivier Clément tells us that "the world was created as an act of celebration, so that we might share in grace and become Eucharist through the offerings of human beings."[12] Does this mean that our substance becomes that of Christ, that the whole world is ultimately transubstantiated? Remembering the dynamics of the Incarnation, I would prefer to put it like this: the creation is to be transformed not into the groom but into his bride. The Eucharist is a wedding, for the sake of which the Son takes flesh and gives himself to us as the bread of life. The goal of this action is not to convert our own substance, like that of the bread, into Christ the head, but to convert it into the Church, his mystical body. It is to make us into "mothers" of the Son, freely bearing him in the ground of the soul as he is born in the ground of the Trinity, the divine nature, where he is eternally at rest even while he is eternally in action.

Notes

1. Ratzinger, *The Spirit of the Liturgy*, 173.
2. Guardini, *Meditations before Mass*, 68.
3. Stein, *The Science of the Cross*, 179.
4. We do not have to hypothesize that the Mass was consciously drawn up with this structure in mind. The reason for the association is quite simple. The Mass is the center of the Church's liturgical life, and if the sacraments are integral to that life, each of them will naturally be reflected within it.

5. The Church's liturgy is described in the Letter to the Hebrews: "But what you have come to is Mount Zion and the city of the living God, the heavenly Jerusalem where the millions of angels have gathered for the festival, with the whole Church in which everyone is a 'first-born son' and a citizen of heaven" (Heb. 12:22–23, JB translation). "The Mass is, actually, a sacramental participation in the liturgy of heaven, the cult officially rendered to the Trinity by the full host of the spiritual creation. The presence of the angels introduces the Eucharist into heaven itself," says Jean Daniélou, SJ, in *The Angels and Their Mission* (62).

6. See *Catechism of the Catholic Church*, paras. 1322–1419, and especially on this point paras. 1374–77.

7. Technically, "accidents" are those incidental properties that exist as properties of, or inhere in, something else which is their "subject."

8. See Schmemann, *For the Life of the World*, 23–46. Another Orthodox writer, Olivier Clément, writes: "Christ, through the priest, fulfills the Eucharist by the memorial. That is the dimension that the Latin Church was to emphasize. Everything is fulfilled in the Holy Spirit for whom the priest asks the Father in close communion with the people. That is the dimension that the Christian East was to emphasize. Two inseparable dimensions are today on the way to reunion after a long history of separation" (*The Roots of Christian Mysticism*, 112).

9. *Introduction to Christianity*, 132. In "Person: Substance and Relation" (*Communio*, Spring 1995, 139–63), John S. Grabowski begins to explore the implications of this statement. On the relational character of substance as understood in an Orthodox Christian perspective see Zizioulas, *Being as Communion*, 84–89.

10. Human beings cannot change material realities ontologically simply by giving them a new meaning. That is what is wrong with theories of "trans-signification" and "transfinalization." God, however, can do so. In fact each of the sacraments, it could be argued, involves an ontological change of some kind, either in the matter of the sacrament itself or in the one who receives it. The ontological reality of a thing is its meaning for God, since its very act of existence is a participation in the act which is God. Substance is an action.

11. Cited in a wonderful collection compiled and edited by Gaudoin-Parker, *The Real Presence through the Ages*, 51.

12. Clément, *The Roots of Christian Mysticism*, 110.

THREE

Initiation
Living the Mysteries

So then you are no longer strangers and sojourners, but you are fellow citizens with the saints and members of the household of God, built upon the foundation of the apostles and prophets, Christ Jesus himself being the chief cornerstone, in whom the whole is joined together and grows into a holy temple in the Lord; in whom you also are built into it for a dwelling place of God in the Spirit.
— Saint Paul (Eph. 2:18–22)

In a well-known book called *Lost Christianity,* Jacob Needleman speculates whether some vital part of Jesus's teaching has gone missing — namely the element that explained how we were actually to be able to live as Christians. Certainly looking at the way Christians have behaved over the centuries — or closer to home, at how we ourselves so often behave — it is hard not to wonder whether he had a point.

In fact there is nothing missing, but there is all the difference in the world between possessing a key and actually turning it in the lock. The sacramental life brings us into the closest possible relation to spiritual forces that can change our lives and transform our existence.

In this book I am concentrating on the number seven as a way of understanding the sacramental life, but other numerical patterns abound in Scripture and tradition — most obviously three, four, ten, twelve, and various combinations of these (seven is three plus four, ten is seven plus three, twelve is three times four, and so on). Three is the most significant of all, since it refers to the Trinity.[1]

Sacraments of Initiation

As mentioned earlier, the seven sacraments break down into one group of three and two groups of two. The group of three includes Baptism, Confirmation, and Eucharist, corresponding in the mystical journey to the three stages of Purification, Illumination, and Union.[2] These are the sacraments of initiation that insert us into the Christian life, the life of the Holy Spirit and of the Church, whereas the other sacraments presume this initiation and have more specialized functions.

There is a fairly obvious association between the three sacraments of initiation and the Holy Trinity. Confirmation is linked by tradition especially to the Holy Spirit, who descended on the disciples at Pentecost, while the Eucharist reveals the specific work of the Son as redeemer of the world. Baptism reveals the work of the Father — for a Christian is "begotten" by God in this sacrament, and a voice from heaven reveals Jesus's relationship to his Father when he is baptized in the Jordan. Before going on to look at the challenges of living this initiation in everyday life and how the sacraments themselves help us with that, let's focus on Baptism.

In the Beginning

Do we think enough about our Baptism? Do we at least recall its significance from time to time, perhaps when we make the sign of the Cross with holy water on entering a church? Baptism is more than being freed from original sin, more than an exorcism (although it is that too). Jesus submitted himself to the Baptism of John in the River Jordan at the outset of his public ministry, and although he did not need it for himself, it was necessary "for the fulfilment of all righteousness" (Matt. 3:15). There is a link between this act and his last act, the words, "It is accomplished" (John 19:30). In the river Jordan, the Spirit descends on Jesus like a dove; on the Cross, the Spirit ascends to the Father, and from the Son's side the life of the Church now flows. In Baptism, we descend with Jesus into the waters of death, to emerge as "sons in the Son," ready for any mission we may receive from the Father. Are we faithfully carrying out that mission today?

After his resurrection, Jesus commissioned the Apostles to teach and baptize all nations. The Church, meditating upon the Baptism that she is commanded to transmit, formulated doctrines about its nature and purpose. Baptism, she tells us (most recently in the *Catechism of the Catholic Church*), is the sacrament that first inserts us into the life of Christ, initiating us into his redemptive death and freeing us from slavery to sin (paras. 1213–14). Baptism is in a very real sense a "second birth" (para. 1215). We are born from heaven in a process made possible by the Holy Spirit.

We are sons, by grace if not by nature, but sons in the real sense, sons that have received a name from the Father. "Beloved, we are God's children now; it does not yet appear what we shall be, but we know that when he appears we shall be like him, for we shall see him as he is. And everyone who thus hopes in him purifies himself as he is pure" (1 John 3:2–3).

Baptism is the beginning of a new life. In the octagonal baptistry that Pope Sixtus III built in the fifth century for the Basilica of Saint John Lateran (the cathedral church of Rome), the following verse was inscribed:

The city, a people to be consecrated,
Here springs into being from fruitful seed
Which the Spirit brings forth from the impregnated waters.
Be dipped in the sacred stream, O sinner called to purity:
Whom the water will receive old, but bring forth new.
There is no distinction among those born again,
Whom one font, one Spirit, one faith make one.
From her virginal womb Mother Church
Gives birth in the stream to her children,
Whom she conceives through the breath of God.
If you would be pure, cleanse yourself in this bath,
Whether you are oppressed by original sin or by your own guilt.
This is the fountain of life, which purges the whole world,
Taking its course from the wound of Christ.
Hope for the Kingdom of Heaven, you who are reborn in this font;
The blessed life does not accept those who are born only once.
Let not the number or the kind of his sins frighten anyone;
Born of the stream he shall be holy.[3]

The "wound of Christ" referred to here is, of course, the one the soldier's lance made in Christ's side as he hung dead upon the Cross: "and immediately there came out blood and water" (John 19:34). The official reason for piercing Christ's heart was to prove his death, but in fact it released what the Church has always understood to be the waters of Baptism (water) and the Eucharist (blood) — for it is by Christ's actual death that Death himself is ultimately defeated. Later the meaning of the wound is completely reversed, when it becomes the proof not of his death but of his resurrection. Jesus asks doubting Thomas to "bring your hand and put it into my side, and be not faithless but faithful" (John 20:27).

Our Lord gives us his own catechesis on the sacrament of Baptism in John's Gospel, chapter 3 (verses 1–15), in his discourse with the Pharisee Nicodemus, who comes to Jesus "by night" to receive instruction in this mystery. Nicodemus asks how it is possible for someone to be born a second time. Jesus replies (and this is echoed in the baptistry verse just quoted) that without a second birth no one can enter the Kingdom. One must be born again "of water and the Spirit," that is, from sacramental water, water in which the Holy Spirit is flowing like an inner fire. The Spirit is God's "breath" (*ruach*): "it blows where it wishes, and you hear the sound of it, but you do not know whence it comes and whither it goes: so it is with everyone who is born of the Spirit," for "what is born of the Spirit is spirit." Our whole persons, including our earthly bodies, must become spirit, must be "spiritualized," to be able to enter the Kingdom of Heaven.

An example of what Jesus means by becoming spirit, or coming and going like the wind, is furnished for us in the Book of Acts, sometime after the baptism of the Holy Spirit had been received at Pentecost (Acts 8:25–40). Philip is brought to an Ethiopian eunuch at the precise moment when he is sitting in his chariot reading the prophecies of Isaiah and wondering what they might mean. Philip explains how they refer to Jesus Christ, and the eunuch asks to be baptized in some water they find by the side of the road. Having baptized him, "the Spirit of the Lord seized Philip, and the eunuch saw him no more," but Philip found himself in Azotus. One has the impression that he did not know how he got there.

Jesus's resurrected body, which comes and goes invisibly and unpredictably, is our model of the new life into which we are reborn through Baptism. The sacrament is the way we participate in Christ's death and resurrection so we may attain our own new existence. Saint Paul's commentary on Baptism can be found in his first letter to the Corinthians (15:29–57). This should be read in conjunction with the conversation with Nicodemus. One further point from that conversation should be remarked upon. At the end of his comments, Jesus adds: "No one has ascended into heaven but he who descended from heaven." This surely implies that it is only *in Jesus,* as part of his resurrected body, that we ourselves will ascend and enter the Kingdom.[4]

Powers of the Christian Soul

How is it then, if Baptism is such a dramatic new birth, the beginning of a brand-new life, that most people who are baptized hardly notice the fact, and there is little if any discernible difference between a Christian and a non-Christian?

In 1 Corinthians 15, Saint Paul's image is that of a seed that is sown in the ground. In part this refers to our eventual physical death, but mainly it refers to our death in Jesus, in Baptism itself, which submerges us in the waters of life. In this earthly life we are *drowning men,* still in the process of dying and being re-born.[5] Until we have definitively become saints, our longed-for rebirth is only virtual, potential, implicit. The process is hidden so deep within us that we may not be aware of it. But that is not to say that we can just relax and let it happen. The process of dying and of being born is always a struggle. It involves our will, it engages our freedom, and it demands our complete commitment. That is why the Christian life requires the practice of virtues.

A "virtue" in the word's original meaning is a *power,* a power of the human soul. (We faintly recall this meaning when we use the expression "by virtue of," for example in the phrase, "by virtue of necessity.") The acquisition of virtues, then, empowers us; it liberates us so we can become more fully what we should be — what God is calling us to be. The negative vortex of selfishness that daily constricts our personality and poisons our relationships can only be reversed with input from a higher sphere, outside ourselves. The powers or virtues that supply that assistance are threefold: faith (the power to believe), hope (the power to trust), and love (the power to receive and to give). These virtues make the process of healing possible. At the same time they open our spiritual senses, enabling us to see the "invisible."[6]

The Mystical Virtues

These three virtues in particular — faith, hope, and love — are called "theological" virtues because they can make us holy, or God-like. (*Theo* means "God" and *logos* means a pattern or design.) Love is the highest of the three virtues, as Saint Paul tells us in a famous passage from 1 Corinthians that ends with the words: "So faith, hope, love abide, these three; but the greatest of these is love." If we were to link each of the theological virtues with one of the sacraments of initiation, faith would seem to fit best with Baptism, our means of entry into the Church, while hope would correspond to Confirmation, which is the sacrament of confidence in the truth that has been revealed. That would align love with the Eucharist, an appropriate enough association since this sacrament is the manifestation and consummation of the Son's saving love. The Eucharist is the fulfillment to which Baptism and Confirmation look forward, and the Father and Holy Spirit support this completion of the Son's mission.

G. K. Chesterton, in his inimitable way, summed up the difference between paganism and Christianity by contrasting these three "virtues of grace," as he called them, with the pagan, or natural, virtues commonly called "cardinal" (the cardinal virtues will be examined in more detail in a moment). He writes that "The pagan, or rational, virtues are such things as justice and temperance, and Christianity has adopted them. The three mystical virtues which Christianity has not adopted, but invented, are faith, hope and charity" (he uses the more archaic word for love based on the Latin *caritas*). He notes that the pagan virtues are "sad" whereas the mystical virtues are "gay and exuberant." The pagan virtues are "reasonable," the Christian virtues "as unreasonable as they can be," for: "Justice consists in finding out what is due to a certain man and giving it to him. Temperance consists in finding out the proper limit of a particular indulgence and adhering to that. But charity means pardoning what is unpardonable, or it is no virtue at all. Hope means hoping when things are hopeless, or it is no virtue at all. And faith means believing the incredible, or it is no virtue at all."[7]

Thus, he adds, the more unreasonable virtues are also the most "practical," since it is when we are most in need and most undeserving that we stand most in need of charity, and it is in the hopeless moment that we have most need of the hopeful man.

The Evangelical Counsels

While we are thinking about the three mystical virtues, it is worth noting that they can be connected with another interesting triad in the Christian tradition. This is the triad of what Christianity has termed the "counsels of perfection," or evangelical counsels. They are based upon the call to exclusive service that Jesus directs in the Gospels to the rich young man whom he loves (see Mark 10:17–31 and Luke 18:18–30).

The counsels have been translated over time into three formal *vows:* Poverty, Chastity, and Obedience. Taking these vows is not a condition of salvation: they define a particular state of life, which is right for some but not for all. The spiritual practice of Christian monks and nuns was first tested and articulated in the Syrian and Egyptian deserts where many of the early Christians fled to seek God.[8] Monks and nuns ever since have sought to separate themselves from the world around them by promising to give up private ownership of any possessions, to refrain from sexual contact, and to submit their will to the head of their monastery or order. In this way they try to live partly, even now, in the world to come. The *spirit* (rather than the letter) of the vows, however, applies not just to those in the religious state but to every Christian, as the *Catechism* informs us: "Christ proposes the evangelical counsels, in their great variety, to every disciple."[9]

These three counsels seem to echo both the theological virtues and also the sacraments of initiation. Poverty (which might also be called detachment) corresponds to the virtue of faith, since it readies us to receive the gift of God, and to the sacrament of Baptism, since in that sacrament we die to the world in order to be reborn by water and the Holy Spirit. Chastity (or purity) corresponds to hope, since it calls us to live in the expectation of a consummation we cannot experience in this present time, and to trust in the invisible that we have grasped by faith. It also corresponds to the sacrament of Confirmation, since this trust is what enables us to witness for our faith even to the point of dying for it.

The third counsel, obedience, needs a word or two more of explanation — especially in the context of modern culture, which is founded on the concept of freedom and recognizes the possible abuses of blind obedience to merely human authority. Traditionally, the promise of obedience is conditional on not being ordered to do anything morally wrong. Obedience is supposed to govern the choices one might make within a fundamentally ethical way of life. The key element is not that you are letting someone else do your thinking for you, but that you are submitting yourself to the order of a community that transcends you.

Vowing obedience means that we are prepared to integrate ourselves into such a higher order, one serving goals beyond our own limited desires, in order to achieve perfection. Obedience to some (legitimate) authority is one useful way of doing this, especially since one of the great obstacles to being healed of our sins is the pride that makes us want to decide every little thing for ourselves. False pride is the basis for a false self. Obedience done in the spirit of humility is an exercise designed to undermine the basis for a false self.

In ordinary life, whether in the home, in school, in politics, or in sport, there are plenty of opportunities for obedience, and in fact the smooth running of society depends upon a certain amount of it. Outside the monastery we may not be told precisely how to organize our day, but we must still submit ourselves to some order that comes from outside ourselves. Ultimately we must find a way to submit ourselves to the order that comes from God and is always in our best interest (however things might seem to contradict this on the surface or in the short term).

Obedience is connected to the virtue of love, for love is the root of spiritual obedience. In the end, we can only submit ourselves in the fullest sense of the word to one whom we love. Love is the only source of true authority in the Christian life, as Jesus showed us by washing the feet of his disciples and by dying on the Cross. Love is also especially associated with the Eucharist, which is often called the sacrament of God's love. In this sacrament our Lord gives himself to us and completes his redeeming work.

Sacraments of Healing and Community

The descriptions of the different counsels and their relationship to the virtues infused into our souls by the Holy Spirit shows us that it is the virtues which *enable us to live the counsels*. Having delved beneath the surface of tradition and discovered some connections between the sacraments of initiation, the theological virtues, and the evangelical counsels, can we make sense of the remaining sacraments in a similar vein? These sacraments are fourfold: Reconciliation and Anointing (the sacraments of healing), Ordination and Marriage (sacraments of community). It is necessary to look now for patterns of four, and in fact we come quickly to another set of virtues that seem to fit the bill.

The Reasonable Virtues

The four *cardinal virtues* (a name derived from the Latin word for hinge, since the ancients taught that the good life "hinges" on these powers) are fortitude (or courage), temperance (or moderation), prudence (a form of wisdom), and justice. Each of these virtues refers to an inner state of balance: being constant in the face of danger, not doing too much of one thing or another, keeping a sense of proportion, treating people (and oneself) fairly. There is nothing particularly Christian about these virtues, as Chesterton noted in the passage just quoted. Christianity took them over from the ancient pagan world, and in fact they probably underlie most systems of morality. These virtues simply describe what it is to achieve a healthy, balanced self. But Christianity supernaturalizes them.

It is, firstly, easy to see how the four cardinal virtues in various ways depend on the theological virtues for their Christian expression — especially on love, which Saint Thomas calls the underlying *form* of all the virtues. In a sense each cardinal virtue depends on love's spirit of obedience:

- Fortitude, the strength of character needed to sustain a decision when things become difficult or painful, is based on submission to God.

- Prudence integrates the self with a wisdom that transcends our own knowledge and experience of what to do or say.

- Temperance tames the self enough to prevent any particular urge from destroying the balance of the whole.

✦ Justice has us submit to a higher order that is fair to all, so
we are able to see, judge, and act without partiality.

Secondly, there are four main ways in which we can *fail* to
transcend ourselves with the help of grace, four ways we can
remain cooped up in our own mess, turned in upon ourselves.
Most of our problems in life can be traced back to one of these
failures. We have been incapacitated by cowardice (the opposite
of fortitude), or been foolish (the opposite of prudent), or been
intemperate and overly self-indulgent (the opposite of temperance), or acted wrongly toward others (the opposite of justice).
Each of the corresponding cardinal virtues heals and stabilizes
one of these key areas of our life, where love is hindered.

Now the question before us is, do the cardinal virtues correspond in any way to the remaining four (non-initiatory)
sacraments? Those sacraments are Reconciliation, Anointing,
Marriage, and Ordination. In fact we can make the connections fairly easily.[10] Reconciliation clearly aligns with justice.
The sacrament of *Reconciliation*, through confession, absolution,
and penance, restores a state of justice toward God and man.
Anointing is affiliated with fortitude, since it strengthens us for
the final battle of our lives. (These two sacraments, and the
virtues associated with them, involve the healing of the individual, first in his relationship with others and second in his
own right.) *Marriage* aligns with temperance, since it restores
the original balance in our nature between male and female.
Ordination in turn can be linked to prudence, since the priest
is living his submission to the higher order of wisdom, wisdom
that Saint Paul describes as "the foolishness of God," which
is "wiser than men" (1 Cor. 1:25). (These two pairs are sacraments and virtues that serve to build up the community, firstly
the natural community of men and women, and secondly the
community of the Church.)

The relationships we have discussed may be summarized in the following table:

Sacrament	Virtue	Counsel	Trinity
Baptism	Faith	Poverty	Father
Confirmation	Hope	Chastity	Holy Spirit
Eucharist	Love	Obedience	Son
Reconciliation	Justice		
Anointing	Fortitude		
Marriage	Temperance		
Ordination	Prudence		

Patterns of the kind we have been discovering may look trivial, but they help to demonstrate tradition's inner coherence and throw some light on the meaning of a Christian life.

Christian initiation is best understood as a process leading to union with God in the life of the Holy Trinity. The underlying dynamic of a Christian life is therefore necessarily trinitarian. The three dimensions of Christian spirituality which we enter through the sacraments may be described in terms of living the spirit of the three evangelical counsels — poverty, chastity, and obedience. It is very important to realize that the requirement for living in this threefold spirit is not the mastery of some lost, arcane discipline but simply the powers infused within us by the Trinity: faith, hope, and love. We grow in these dimensions of Christian existence through our participation in the three sacraments that initiate us into the divine life.

And from the heart of this Christian existence — from the inner triad, as it were — there then unfold the remaining four sacraments, which depend upon receiving the three sacraments of initiation first. All four of these sacraments are a species of miracle: they represent the life of God bursting into our human world. A classical cardinal virtue that describes the integrated human being is supernaturalized in each of them, creating a new way of human living. It becomes *possible* to forgive and to be forgiven (the sacrament of Reconciliation). It becomes *possible* to face down the last enemy of men and approach even death with equanimity (Anointing). It becomes *possible* to unite oneself completely to another human being and in so doing find one's own integrity (Marriage). It becomes *possible* to live by a wisdom that transcends the world and looks like folly to the eyes of men (Ordination).

Bookstores are filled to overflowing with self-help and personal empowerment titles. Everyone seems to want to know how to become *what they have the potential to be.* They want to achieve more, become happy, be beautiful, be free of whatever they think is holding them back. Yet the richest and most complete teaching on this very subject is to be found in the last place most people would think of looking: in fusty old books of Catholic doctrine on the virtues and the sacraments.

Notes

1. I hope to devote two further books in this series to the mysteries associated with the numbers twelve and three.

2. In *Guénonian Esoterism and Christian Mystery,* chap. 9, "Sacramental Initiation and the Discipline of the Arcane," Borella spends some time examining the sacraments of initiation in greater detail, and I refer the interested reader to his account.

3. Cited by James Francis Cardinal Stafford in the preface to *Rediscovering Baptism* by the Pontifical Council for the Laity (6).

4. Daniélou (*The Bible and the Liturgy,* 118) explains the close relationship of Baptism and Confirmation thus: "In the same way as Baptism configures us to Christ dead and risen again, so Confirmation configures us to Christ anointed by the Holy Spirit. The Baptism of Christ, followed by the descent of the Spirit, is thus seen to be a prefiguration of His death followed by His royal enthronement, of which the Christian in turn partakes by means of the two sacraments of water and the anointing."

5. "Do you not know that all of us who have been baptized into Christ Jesus were baptized into his death? We were buried therefore with him by

baptism, so that as Christ was raised from the dead by the glory of the Father, we too might walk in newness of life" (Rom. 6:3–4).

6. A line from the chorus of a popular song by K. T. Tunstall captures this quite well: "The power to be, the power to give, the power to see, yeah yeah ... " Thus the virtues are also powers that make possible the spiritual interpretation of Scripture, faith corresponding to the allegorical meaning of the text, hope to the anagogical meaning, and love to the tropological or moral meaning. (See Tavard, *Transiency and Permanence*, 47–49.)

7. Chesterton, *Heretics*, 124–25.

8. The retreat of Jesus to the wilderness for forty days of fasting after his baptism by John has always been a model for Christians, and in fact the three temptations that the Gospel records Christ defeated there represent the whole range of temptations to which human flesh is subject: temptations against, precisely, faith, hope, and love, and also against poverty, chastity, and obedience.

9. *Catechism of the Catholic Church*, n. 915.

10. Saint Bonaventure (*Breviloquium*, 181) puts it like this: "Baptism restores one to [spiritual] health and disposes one for faith, confirmation for hope, the Eucharist for charity, penance for justice, extreme unction for perseverance which is the complement and summation of bravery, holy orders for prudence, and matrimony for the preservation of temperance which the weakness of our flesh particularly needs but the righteousness of marriage remedies."

Pillars of Wisdom

This section synthesizes some reflections on some of the sets of seven that we find in holy Scripture, reading them in the light and spirit of Catholic tradition. The purpose is to encourage a multidimensional scriptural meditation on the sacraments.

As explained at the end of the first chapter, there are five main sets of seven that we will focus on here. These include Jesus's seven last words from the Cross, the seven petitions or requests that make up the Lord's Prayer, and the seven days of creation from the Book of Genesis. In addition there are two sets of seven drawn specifically from the Gospel of John. These are known to biblical scholars as the seven "signs" (miracles recorded by John as representing different aspects of Jesus's mission), and the seven "I am" sayings (phrases in which Jesus combined a reference to the divine name revealed to Moses with a symbolic title for himself). These have been arranged in clusters according to the sacrament to which they seem to correspond, with a commentary bringing out some of the significant points. (A bare list of headings without the accompanying commentary will be found at the end of the chapter for ease of reference.)

Marriage
Coming of the Kingdom

Marriage is a sacrament (an effective sign of grace) by virtue of its connection with the archetypal marriage of Christ and his Church, which glorifies the Father and establishes his Kingdom. In a sacramental human marriage, each lays down their life for the other, as Christ did for us. This is a way of participating directly in the Son's self-sacrifice, and of sharing in the joy and fruitfulness of his eternal victory over death.

First Sign Changing Water into Wine (John 2:1–11)

The number of miracles recorded in the Gospel of John (the most obviously sacramentally or liturgically minded of the four Evangelists) may be as many as nine, if you include the Resurrection and the miraculous draught of fishes that follows it. Yet those that lead up to the supreme miracle of the Resurrection are exactly seven.

The first miracle John relates takes place at a wedding celebration at Cana in Galilee. The wine having run out, Mary brings the problem to her son's attention. His immediate reaction seems strange: "Woman [perhaps better translated as Lady, or Madam], what is that to thee or to me? My Hour is not yet come." Nevertheless, Mary commands the servants, "Do whatever he tells you," and indeed Jesus brings about the desired miracle, by asking for six stone jars to be filled with water and then turning the water into wine. In this way, John says, Jesus "manifested his glory." The miracle, of course, does more than focus our attention on the grace that comes through Marriage. Reference to the "hour" that has not yet come — the hour of the Passion — connects Marriage to the Cross, but also implicitly to the Kingdom that is to come.

James Mensch[1] has pointed out that John often employs double meanings, and by an ambiguity in the Greek, the words "Jesus and his disciples were invited" could also mean "Jesus and his disciples were celebrated." The hint that Mensch picks up on is that Jesus and his Church are the real bridegroom and bride. The "servants" who fill the jars for Jesus, Mensch points out, are literally "ministers" or "deacons." The stone jars that are filled "to the brim" (a word that could also mean "above" or "in heaven") were used "for the Jewish rites of purification" — but they are standing empty, awaiting the greater rites of the new covenant.

"I Am the True Vine" (John 15:1)

Just as the seven signs seem to unfold aspects of the one miracle that is the life, love, and resurrection of Jesus Christ, so Jesus's "I am" sayings seem to unfold aspects of the divine name.

The "I am" saying that we can most easily link with Marriage occurs during the Last Supper: "I am the true vine, and my Father is the vinedresser." The immediate context is the need to "bear fruit," fruit that "abides." By such fruit the Father is glorified. But in order to bear fruit, the disciples must "abide in my love" and "love one another," that "my joy may be in you, and that your joy may be full."

"Greater love has no man than this, that a man lay down his life for his friends." The discourse continues (verses 2–17), and its subject is *friendship:* "No longer do I call you servants [slaves]...but I have called you friends." There is no explicit mention of that supreme type of friendship known as marriage, in which a man and a woman lay down their life for one another. However, we recall that traditionally the Last Supper is known as the wedding feast of the Lamb, and certainly Jesus's reference to the fullness of joy introduces a note of celebration or festival. Furthermore, the emphasis on fruitfulness through a complete giving of self speaks to the very essence of marriage. What we have here, in fact, is a series of instructions on Christ's "marriage" to his disciples.

Seventh Day **The Sabbath**

Why should the seven signs correspond to the seven days of creation *in reverse order,* as they are listed here?[2] Perhaps because they circle closer and closer to the great mystery of Easter itself, in which they are all implicitly contained, and the Resurrection is the new creation. It is at the end of Christ's earthly life that we find the new beginning of all things.

The seventh day of creation in the Book of Genesis, the Sabbath, is the furthest from the beginning. It is the day of completion, of God's rest and blessing, and the anticipation of his final kingdom. It is also, in Jewish tradition, fittingly called the day of God's "wedding," for it is the day God seals his relationship with the created world. The whole world has, through man, been brought to the condition of maturity in freedom, and it can now enjoy its Creator's love. The six stone jars of John 2:1–11 (representing the six days of God's activity in Genesis) are full. This is the festival day of the marriage between God and the world, the day when the waters over which the Spirit of God hovered in the very beginning become wine, to bring the work of the six days to perfection.[3]

"Woman, Behold Your Son" (John 19:25–27)

There are only two places where John has recorded for us that Jesus addresses his mother as "Woman." The first is at the wedding at Cana; the second is when he speaks from the Cross. Jesus sees her standing near "the disciple whom he loved" and says to her, "Woman, behold your son!" To the disciple he says, "Behold your mother!" and "from that hour the disciple took her to his own home," or (literally) "into the things that were his."

This word from the Cross, according to Adrienne von Speyr, concerns the relation not merely of son to mother, but of man to woman. Age is irrelevant. A man is being given to a woman and vice versa. Both are virgins and will remain so; therefore it does not matter that they belong to different generations. The bonding of a man to a woman does not require the loss of virginity, as we see in the virginal but valid marriage of Mary to Joseph.

Mary is not, of course, being "married" to the disciple John. Like many of the Church Fathers, Adrienne identifies the gift of John to Mary as giving her a son in place of Jesus. This is the beginning of the Church. In taking John as her son, she becomes a universal Mother; from now on, she will have to accept anyone her Son gives her. Her motherhood is raised even higher: henceforth, as Mother at the Cross, she is Mother to the Church for all eternity. The Spirit who once overshadowed her womb does so again in a new way at the Lord's wish; she will not bear another child in her womb, but she will accept her Son's spiritual child — his love's disciple — as her own son. John is "placed at the centre of the Cross's fruitfulness"; he represents every Christian who receives Mary as his Mother by joining himself to the Body of Christ. The "marriage" in question here, once again, is the archetypal marriage between Christ and his bride the Church. This is the divine aspect of the sacrament of Marriage to which Saint Paul refers as "a great mystery" (Eph. 5:32).

"Thy Kingdom Come"

The prayer of prayers that we call the Our Father or the Lord's Prayer is made up of seven requests or petitions. Jesus gave these to the disciples when they requested to be taught to pray (Matt. 6:9–13). "After we have placed ourselves in the presence of God our Father to adore and to love and to bless him, the

Spirit of adoption [sonship] stirs up in our hearts seven petitions, seven blessings. The first three, more theologal [*sic*], draw
us toward the glory of the Father; the last four, as ways toward
him, commend our wretchedness to his grace. 'Deep calls to
deep' (Psalm 42:8)."[4] Since the true answer to each and every
prayer is ultimately the Lord himself, and since it is through the
Church's sacraments that Christ intends to give himself to us,
we might expect to find each of the sacraments at least loosely
corresponding to one of the Petitions.

The coming of the kingdom is the great moment of eschatological fulfillment. The kingdom or reign to which we look
forward is the full uniting of the person of Jesus with that of
his bride, the Church. The human marriage of husband and
wife, together with their children, forms a living icon of the
kingdom that is "not of this world." Recalling the royal dignity
of marriage, the Orthodox Liturgy crowns the couple at their
wedding ceremony. For all these reasons, this particular petition
corresponds most closely to the sacrament of Marriage.

Baptism
Giving of the Name

*Baptism inserts us into the life of Christ by initiating us into his re-
demptive death, potentially freeing us from slavery to sin. The Spirit in
whom the Son submits himself to the Father's will makes possible our
own new birth from heaven. We are reborn into an identity determined
by the new mission or Christian name we receive from the second Adam,
who is the new father of the human race.*

In Scripture much is made of *names* and the process of *naming*.
Both the Old and New Testaments are full of it, right down
to Simon's receiving the name Peter in recognition of his role
as the rock on which the Church is to be founded, and the

changing of Saul's name to Paul. In the book of Revelation we are promised a "new name" (2:17). It is clear that in the Jewish tradition, giving a name was equivalent to defining an identity or role. Names had *power;* they were not just arbitrary labels stuck on for the sake of convenience. The disciples were taught to cast out demons "in the name of Jesus"; apparently using the name, backed up by prayer and fasting, was supposed to accomplish the exorcism. The fact that Joseph gave Jesus his name, *even though he was not the boy's biological father,* meant that in Jewish law Joseph was the father and Jesus his son. The father gives a name, and the name accords a place in society. Being given a new Christian name at Baptism is similarly significant. Essentially, in Baptism we are being reborn in a *new identity* determined by the mission that we receive from Christ.

Second Sign Healing the Official's Son (John 4:46–54)

John's Gospel describes the second sign as follows: "So he came again to Cana in Galilee, where he had made the water wine. And at Capernaum there was an official whose son was ill." The official asks Jesus to cure his son. Jesus, still seeing a weakness in the man's faith, replies to the effect, "Unless you people see signs and wonders, you will not believe." But the man is able to respond with a direct, heartfelt appeal: "Sir, come down before my child dies." Jesus answers, "Go, your son lives." The man believes him even before the evidence is given, but he confirms his faith when his servants meet him on the way home and tell him that the child has been cured: "the fever left him" in the very hour that Jesus had spoken. The man "and all his household" are converted.

Of course, the Church Fathers often took a fever to represent the state of sin: the son in the story may therefore be taken to represent humanity brought low by the fall, and then raised up by Jesus to a state of grace. But our real clue that this sign concerns the inner meaning of the sacrament of Baptism in particular is provided by its position in the Gospel at the culmination of a series of incidents, each of which deals with some important aspect of that sacrament: the night conversation with Nicodemus, the dispute between a Jew and the followers of John the Baptist over purification, and the meeting with the Samaritan woman at the well. Thus this healing brings to a close a cycle of teachings that begins with the first cleansing of the temple (John 2:13–22). From all of this we see that Baptism involves cleansing, repentance, second birth, and implanting a new life.

Baptism is also about *fatherhood*. At the center of the miracle is the relationship between a man and the son he has both begotten and named. But the man, having been instrumental in giving life to his son, is powerless to restore it. True fatherhood, the ability to give life and mission, belongs to God, after whom "all fatherhood is named." But it is through the mediation and intercession of others (including our godparents and natural parents) that we receive the sacramental healing of Baptism.

"I Am the Way, and the Truth, and the Life; No One Comes to the Father, Except through Me" (John 14:6)

This is said in answer to Thomas, who asks, "Lord, we do not know where you are going; how do we know the way?" It is therefore about *initiation* in the way: the way to the truth, to life in and from the truth. Baptism, being the sacrament of initiation in which we receive our Christian name, is also suggested in the same passage of the Gospel by the words to Philip: "If you ask anything *in my name*, I will do it" (v. 13). Verse 17 then leads into the promise of the in-dwelling Spirit — the giving of whom to the baptized is one of the defining characteristics of this sacrament.

Sixth Day Adam and Eve

As described in the book of Genesis, the sixth day of creation is the day on which the Lord God brings forth the living creatures of the land "according to their kinds" and Adam to have dominion over them. It is the day of God's fatherhood of man and of man's being given fatherhood over creation. It is also the day of naming, according to the second account of the creation (Gen. 2:4–25). First the animals, and finally Woman, receive their names (that is to say, their true role or mission in the creation) from "the Adam," who is placed in the Garden of Eden as God's steward. The world newly created, in other words, is now baptized. Today in the sacrament of Baptism it is we who are brought to Christ — the second Adam — to be named as members of his new creation.

"It Is Accomplished" (John 19:30)

The completion of the Passion (and thus of the Incarnation) is the true foundation of the sacrament of Baptism. As the first of the sacraments of initiation, Baptism inserts us within the body of Christ, joining us definitively and irrevocably to the human nature of the Son of God. But the human nature to which we are united by the sacrament is a human nature *in the very act of being "poured out" for others.* "Do you not know," Saint Paul writes, "that as many as were baptized into Christ Jesus were baptized into his death? We were buried therefore with him through Baptism into death, so that as Christ was raised from the dead through the glory of the Father, so we also might walk in newness of life" (Rom. 6:3–4).

In her little book *The Cross,* Adrienne von Speyr writes: "What seems to be the end to the dying man on the Cross is in fact the opening of his life to all times in the Church, the opening of his finally accomplished life. However Christian life may develop through the centuries, nothing can be added to the fullness of the Son's accomplished work; it can only reveal how rich that accomplishment was." The moment he pronounces these words is the moment he completes his own mission, his own name ("Jesus" means "God saves"). This is the hour he draws all men to himself. His earthly life completed, it is handed over to the Father and to the Church: "He bowed his head and handed over his Spirit." And it is handed over to us at Baptism.

"Our Father, Who Art in Heaven, Hallowed Be Thy Name"

The first of the seven petitions is not a request on our own behalf, but expresses our tribute to the God who created us on the sixth day and who re-creates us on the Cross. We say, essentially, "May thy name be kept sacred, be blessed, be praised, be glorified." This reorientation of the creature in relation to its maker is the foundation of Christian life. We humble ourselves in the dust before God in the heavens. This is Baptism of the heart: turning away from self, "making straight the way of the Lord." And the Father, who is in heaven, allows his sacred name, his *Word*, to be spoken on earth — to be incarnated in the womb of the Church as it was in the womb of Mary. At the moment when Jesus gives up his Spirit on the Cross, that Word has at last been fully spoken. There on the Cross it is hallowed and glorified. Through Baptism we are incorporated within that Word in its earthly expression. Through Baptism, God becomes truly our Father as well as our Creator.

Reconciliation
Unveiling of Sin

Reconciliation is a sacrament for those who have already been baptized into the life of Christ and thus set free from ignorant complicity in

Adam's sin, yet who have repeated that sin consciously in their own name. A sin can be forgiven only by a conscious act of confession, drawing anew on the grace of Baptism. Confession enables us to expose sin for what it is, to detach ourselves from and renounce it; Jesus on the Cross made this possible, as he "became sin for us."

Third Sign Healing the Paralyzed Man (John 5:1–14)

"Now there is in Jerusalem by the Sheep Gate a pool, in Hebrew called Bethsaida, which has five porticoes." When the water in the pool is stirred it is said to have healing properties. Jesus asks a man who has been ill for thirty-eight years, unable to get to the water, "Do you want to be healed?" The man explains he cannot get to the water in time, whereupon Jesus heals him: "Rise, take up your pallet, and walk."

Here the Lord's word, a well of living waters, takes over from the healing waters of Jerusalem. The paralysis the man suffers from symbolizes the state of impotence to which we are reduced by sin (cf. Rom. 7:15–25). As if to reinforce our impression that this sign concerns the inner meaning of Reconciliation, the narrative continues: "Afterwards, Jesus found him in the Temple and said to him, 'Behold! You have become whole; sin no longer, lest something worse befall you.'" And it is surely not irrelevant that the following discourse, provoked by the fact that the healing took place on the Sabbath, includes these words concerning God's forgiveness: "The Father judges no one, but has given all judgment to the Son.... He who hears my word and believes him who has sent me has eternal life, and comes not into judgment but has passed over out of death into life" (verses 22–24).

"I Am the Door" (John 10:9)

"I am the door [gate] of the sheep. All who came before me are thieves and robbers; but the sheep did not hear them. I am the door; if anyone enters through me, he will be saved, and will go in and go out and find pasture." Jesus is speaking to some Pharisees, and he has just accused them in the following terms: "If you were blind, you would not be guilty of sin; but now that you say 'We see,' your guilt remains." (If they in fact see, it cannot be said that "they know not what they do.") He tries to explain what he means with this parable of sheep, thieves, door, and shepherd. He who enters the sheepfold by the door is the shepherd, who can call the sheep by name, for they know his voice. A watchman or doorkeeper must first open the fold to him, and this is the Father. Then the shepherd passes through the gate — Jesus — to lead the sheep. (Jesus is also a shepherd; see below.) As the gate, Jesus is completely in his Father's hands. Here, surely, is another connection with Reconciliation, as Jesus transmits the power of the "keys of the sheepfold" to Peter and the other apostles. And in Reconciliation we pass through the Cross to be saved.

Fifth Day Life Stirring the Waters

Five porticoes surrounded the pool.[5] In our reverse pilgrimage through Genesis, we have come to the fifth day of creation, the day when God created the first self-moving creatures: the fish in the waters and the winged birds. The man at the pool wanted to descend into the waters when they were stirring with life, but he could not, because of his weakness. He wanted to come to the source of life and movement; but now that source comes to him in the flesh, the very God who creates and restores life.

"Father, Forgive Them, for They Know Not What They Do" (Luke 23:34)

According to Adrienne von Speyr (*The Cross*), "This first of the Lord's words [from the Cross] contains his whole life's purpose.

He hangs on the Cross in order to achieve for sinners their forgiveness before God." Jesus has lived among men, "He knows that they cannot be held fully responsible, and the conclusion he draws is this: *he* will bear the responsibility *himself.*" Someone must bear it, so the second Adam assumes the first Adam's office and responsibility in order to make amends for our sin with his own body. But by this very act, sin stands forth unveiled. Those who recognize Jesus as divine can see what their sins are doing to God — mutilating truth, beauty, and goodness. In the mirror of the Cross, they see what they have become. They are no longer ignorant; they know what they do. At the same time, they see how much the Son has done for them, and this moves them to respond with a love that reunites their wills with his. In the act of becoming aware of what they were doing, they cease to do it. This process — the unveiling sin, recognizing self, and loving God — lies at the heart of the sacrament of Reconciliation.

"Forgive Us Our Trespasses, As We Forgive Those Who Trespass against Us"

In the Greek of the New Testament, the word we normally translate as "trespasses" is more accurately rendered "debts" (Matt. 6:12). But what debt is involved in sin, and what light does this cast on the nature of God's forgiveness? One of Saint Francis of Assisi's admonitions suggests an answer: "For the person eats of the tree of the knowledge of good who appropriates to himself his own will, and thus exalts himself over the good things which the Lord says and does in him; and thus, through the suggestion of the devil and the transgression of the command, what he eats becomes for him the fruit of the knowledge of evil." The essence of sin is what we appropriate, what does not belong to us: not an apple, but *our own wills.* It is God who creates my will; my will belongs to him; I *owe* it to him.[6]

A sin, then, is a debt we owe to God, but one that we cannot pay back, for we are bankrupt. We cannot pay our own debts; all we can do is forgive the debts of others against ourselves. But we could not do even that if the Son had not been the *first* to forgive those who trespassed against him; he forgives us and asks the Father to do the same. The forgiveness, the Son's love, is his gift to us, which, if we receive it, we may use to forgive others. It is part of our slavery to sin that we are not free to forgive. Instead, we blame another in order to excuse ourselves (Gen. 3:12–13), and we resent any suffering that is imposed on us as unfair.

In order to receive the Lord's gift of mercy, we must first — like the Good Thief — acknowledge his justice. In order to receive absolution, we must come to the Cross through the sacraments of Baptism and Reconciliation.

Eucharist
Bread of Heaven

The Eucharist is the central sacrament, connecting earth with heaven. Baptism admits us to the body of Christ, but the Eucharist is that body. By Baptism and Reconciliation our sins are forgiven, but the Eucharist is that sacrifice from which they draw that power. Ordination is founded upon it, and for its sake; Confirmation empowers us as its public witnesses; Anointing applies its healing power to us. In the Eucharist, the marriage of heaven and earth is anticipated and effected, and human marriages receive their blessing as the foundation of Christian society.

Fourth Sign Feeding the Five Thousand (John 6:1–15)

This is the fourth in John's carefully constructed series of seven signs. It is therefore the centerpiece of the series, with three signs coming before and three after. A great deal could be said about feeding a vast crowd with five loaves and two fish. But despite all that has been written on this topic through the centuries, there remains a sense of infinite depths below the surface of the text, of mysteries still unspoken. Why are we told precisely *five* loaves? Perhaps because there are five thousand men. But is this an accurate count or another symbolic number? Perhaps it is both. Why two fish? Fish live in water, so perhaps this is a veiled reference to the Eucharist in its second form, as drink — water mixed with wine. (Jesus on the Cross, you could say, thirsts like a fish on dry land.) Another interpretation might be that in the Gospel, fish clearly represent Christians, the catch of the apostles who have become fishers of men. Understood in this way, the miracle is telling us that the community of Christians is multiplied by the same miracle by which they are fed with bread from heaven. In other words, the Eucharist makes the Church. We remember, too, the post-resurrection breakfast described in the last chapter of the Gospel: there, Jesus supplies the bread and some of the fish, but the apostles are able to bring their own catch to the fire.

After the five thousand have eaten, the scraps are gathered into twelve baskets. We still receive the Eucharist in the form of bread from these "baskets" of the twelve apostles, continually replenished for us in the miracle of the Mass.

"I Am the Bread of Life" (John 6:35–71)

The crowds are asking Jesus for a sign. Perhaps they are wondering whether the miracle they have just witnessed was intended to announce his mission as the new great prophet (John 6:14). Moses fed the people with manna in the wilderness; so, it seems, can Jesus. But Jesus responds in a way that confuses them: "I am the bread of life; he who comes to me shall not hunger, and he who believes in me shall never thirst." He presses them further: "This," he says (presumably indicating his own body with a gesture), "is the bread which comes down from heaven, that one may eat and not die...the bread which I will give for the life of the world is my flesh.... He who eats my flesh and drinks my blood abides in me, and I in him. As the living Father sent me, and I live because of the Father, so he who eats me will live because of me."

Many of his followers turn away, shocked by the literal cannibalism that Jesus seems to be advocating, so contrary to what they understand of the law of Moses. To his disciples, Jesus adds: "Do you take offence at this? Then what if you were to see the Son of man ascending to where he was at first? It is the spirit that gives life, the flesh is of no avail; the words that I have spoken to you are spirit and life." The very words he has just spoken, in all their literal force, are spirit and life. In the incarnation of the Word, flesh and spirit, letter and spirit, are held together in an unbreakable bond. Jesus's flesh is not to be eaten separately from the Spirit that gives it life (as would be the case in actual cannibalism). It is to be eaten *while still alive* and without causing death: a miracle that will only be possible after the Ascension and in the Mass. Jesus is really asking, Will you still find it shocking to have to eat my flesh after you have seen me ascend, alive and whole forever, to my Father's side?

Jesus's disciples were asked to take his words on trust. Their full meaning would become clear only later. Today, they illuminate the mystery of the Eucharist and of communion.

Fourth Day Creating the Sun

The fourth day of creation is the day of the sun, the moon, and the stars. It is the day of the creation of cosmic time, regulated and expressed by the movements of the heavenly bodies. Symbolically, it is the day of the creation of *liturgical* time, the Church's year, which revolves around the sacraments. At the center of the seven sacraments, the Eucharist illuminates the spiritual world like a sun, and the "moon" of Scripture in the Liturgy of the Word — shining by the reflected light of the Lord's real presence among his people — prepares the eyes and the congregation's hearts for the coming of the daystar upon the altar. (This symbolism is most fully apparent during Exposition, when the Blessed Sacrament is exposed on the altar for adoration.)

"I Thirst" (John 19:28)

The Son thirsts for us to be filled; his thirst matches in degree the void that surrounds him, the void that he has taken into himself. "Because he emptied himself until his whole self was nothing but a burning void, we possess him in us as Eucharist" (von Speyr, *The Cross*, 47).

A man dying on a cross would not feel hungry, but thirsty. This Word consequently refers to the Eucharist in the appearance of wine. It also refers to the mystery of the distinction of the species: the fact that the bread and the wine are consecrated separately (though not independently) within the Mass. This symbolic separation of blood from body on the altar suggests the same mystery as the words "I thirst." The Lord's physical dehydration anticipates the outpouring of blood and water from his pierced heart in death (John 19:34), an outpouring of his substance into the sacraments themselves. In ancient iconography, the precious blood is frequently shown in the act of being caught by our Lady or by an angel in a chalice or grail. This vessel represents both the cup used in the Mass, and the Church herself; it is the womb of the Church our mother, or the heart of the bride.

"Give Us This Day Our Daily Bread"

We are told that the original meaning of the word *epiousos*, translated here as "daily," is unknown; it has never been found used in another context.[7] Jerome translated it as "supersubstantial" in Matthew and "daily" in Luke. Tradition has taken it to refer both to the food we need to sustain life and (perhaps primarily) to the bread that comes down from heaven of John 6:41, the "bread of life" himself.

This is one of those cases where, if we are trying to connect each of the seven signs with one of the sacraments, there is not much room to maneuver. We couldn't very well argue that this petition tells us about the sacrament of Anointing or Reconciliation. The exciting thing about working out this series is the way each piece falls into place. By process of elimination one arrives at the less obvious correspondences, and then it turns out they really do reveal something about the sacrament in question!

Ordination
Between Heaven and Earth

A priest is consecrated to offer sacrifice on the community's behalf, to reconcile the community with an invisible God (Heb. 5:1). The Christian priest is called to offer the perfect sacrifice of Christ, which is Christ himself. He stands alone, between heaven and earth, the one refuge in the storm of the world. He gathers his flock by accepting, if need be, to be forsaken by all.

Fifth Sign Walking on Water (John 6:19)[8]

The fifth sign in John's sequence intertwines the mystery of Ordination with that of the Eucharist: the walking on water takes place after feeding the five thousand and before the discourse on bread from heaven. In the dark and the wind, with no land in sight, the disciples see Jesus walking across the Sea of Galilee toward Capernaum. They are frightened, and he reassures them with the words: "It is I," or, literally, "I am, do not fear" (v. 20). (The equivalent passage in the Gospel of Matthew tells us that Peter, when called by Jesus, is able to walk over the water too, until he "sees the wind" and is afraid and begins to sink.) Christ, as mediator between heaven and earth, is able to bring the peace of heaven to the turbulent elements below. The very things of which the disciples are afraid — the waves driven by the wind — seem to become a path beneath his feet.[9] It is the familiar sound of his voice, when he gives his name, that calms his flock's fear in the boat (a symbol of the Church).

"I Am the Good Shepherd" (John 10:11)

This saying is found in close proximity to "I am the door" (linking the sacrament of Ordination as closely to that of Reconciliation as the position of the preceding sign seems to link it to the Eucharist). The shepherd calls the sheep by name, and they recognize the sound of his voice; they obey when he calls and follow him. He is not a hireling, but the rightful owner. Christians may think of the priests of the Mosaic Covenant as hirelings, because they did not themselves own the sheep. Their animal sacrifices, in the end, could not take away sin (Heb. 10:4). They could not save the sheep from the wolf, being themselves afraid for their own lives. But Jesus is prepared to lay down his life out of love for his sheep. Not only that, but he has "power to take it again" (John 10:18). By means of his offering, not of the blood of bulls and goats but of his will to the Father, "he has perfected for all time those who are sanctified" (Heb. 10:8–14).

Third Day Land in the Midst of the Waters

On the third day, God gathers the waters into one place, which he calls "seas," and makes dry land appear. From the earth he calls forth vegetation — the trees and plants that grow between earth and heaven. If we think back again to the fifth sign, we find Jesus there presenting himself as the true land to which the disciples are journeying. Not only is he himself dry land in the midst of the raging waters, but when the disciples take him on board, "the boat was immediately at the land to which they were going."

"My God, Why Have You Forsaken Me?" (Mark 15:34)

A man cries out to God. In Christ, the ultimate fruit of Adam's sin is tasted. Adam hid from God among the vegetation created on the third day; now that Jesus is naked, he cannot find his Father. The heart of our Lord's mission is expressed in the words of the 22nd Psalm: "I am poured out like water, and all my bones are out of joint; my heart is like wax, it is melted within my breast...." Jesus goes to the farthest extremity to reclaim the sheep that have been lost; he finds man in his utmost despair and turns him back to the Father, "for he has not despised or abhorred the affliction of the afflicted; he has not hid his face from him, but has heard, when he cried to him." The same Psalm continues, "Yea, to him shall all the proud of the earth bow down.... The afflicted shall eat and be satisfied."

In Adrienne von Speyr's commentary, "The priest utters this 'Why?' when at last he fails to join heaven and earth together in his work, when he can see no way forward, when his weakness becomes too great, and the sin of the world too strong, and nothing has the power to combat it, and there is nothing left but his priestly service which has become meaningless and impotent.... The Son's cry is a prophecy, an anticipation, bearing *in advance* all that will happen to those who are his, who really belong to him, taking seriously the risk of discipleship — all those who were willing to dedicate themselves and now find themselves faced with the void, because they chose the void out of love for mankind."

"Thy Will Be Done on Earth As It Is in Heaven"

The third petition of the Lord's Prayer concerns the mediation between heaven and earth that is the priest's special role and calling.[10] In a more general sense, man is the priest of creation, offering praise on behalf of all creatures to their maker "on earth as it is in heaven." It is by doing the Father's *will* — by making his will our own — that we can each contribute to making earth more like heaven.

Christian mysticism does not aim at union with some impersonal absolute. The Incarnation revealed that God is love: three distinct persons with one undivided will in one divine nature. We become one with God not by ceasing to be ourselves, but precisely by *being* ourselves, by making his will our own. As God and man, Jesus possesses two wills, but his will as man is to do the will of his Father: "My food is to do the will of him who sent me, and to accomplish his work" (John 4:34). On the Mount of Olives before his crucifixion, Jesus prays, "not my will, but thine be done" (Luke 22:42). This act of obedience dictated by love — an act of *human* obedience performed by a divine person — lies at the foundations of Jesus's priesthood, securing us "an eternal redemption," joining earth to heaven by the Tree of the Cross (Heb. 8:9).

It is Christ's unique high priesthood that Ordination transmits sacramentally. The sacrament of Holy Orders provides us with an opportunity at every Mass to place ourselves in the position of Mary in Luke 1:38, whose *fiat* ("May it be to me according to thy word") is, for all time, the perfect human echo of the divine priestly act.[11]

Confirmation
Witness to the Light

The ambiguity of the English word "witness" serves well to bring out the double aspect of Confirmation. The sacrament enables us both to be witnesses because we have witnessed, and to be seen because we have been illuminated by the light of the world. In order to discern and represent Christ, we need the gifts of the Holy Spirit: wisdom, understanding, counsel, knowledge, fortitude, piety, and fear of the Lord. The Holy Spirit, given to us "secretly" or interiorly at Baptism, is given more openly and publicly at Confirmation, as he was given to the early Church at Pentecost.

Sixth Sign Healing the Man Born Blind (John 9:1–40)
and
"I Am the Light of the World" (John 9:5)

Jesus has just openly proclaimed his divinity: "Before Abraham was, I AM" (John 8:58). Of the man who is to be healed, he has said, "It was not that this man sinned, or his parents, but that the works of God might be made manifest in him" (John 9:3). This "making manifest" is one of the most important themes in the following account.

In order to heal the man, Jesus spits on the ground and makes clay to anoint the man's eyes, sending him then to wash in the pool of Siloam (which, John makes sure to tell us, means "sent"), after which the man returns seeing. The anointing is reminiscent of Confirmation, which in the East is still called "chrismation" after the oil of chrism.[12] (In the West, there has been more emphasis on the laying on of hands, although the anointing is still given. A vestige of the anointing remains in Baptism, with which Confirmation was once conjoined.) The emphasis on "sending" recalls the theme of "mission," which is an essential dimension of the adult life of every Christian and is associated especially with the Holy Spirit.

The sacrament of Confirmation thus imposes an obligation to witness to Christ, to spread and defend the faith. At the same time, it gives us the strength to carry out this obligation. It both enlightens the mind and fortifies the will. Thus in the drama that follows the miracle, we see the man's parents telling the Pharisees that they do not know how their son has come to see: "He is of age, ask him." When the Pharisees quiz the man himself, they receive a bold (indeed sassy) answer: "Why do you want to hear it again? Do you too want to become his disciples?" The man has become an adult witness, capable of answering back to his interrogators.

Second Day Creating the Sky

On the second day of creation God makes a firmament called "heaven" or "sky" to separate the waters above and below. By separating the waters, God is creating a space in the world for the wind, the *ruach* or God's "breath" — in other words for sending the Holy Spirit into the world. The sky is also a symbol of *vision:* a great expanse of light and distance. The waters below are able to reflect the waters above because they have been separated from them: the material world reflects or images the spiritual world.

The facts that John's corresponding sign involved the restoration — or creation — of sight in a blind man, and that this was done by spitting on the ground (from the waters above to the waters below, as it were), and that the man washed in the pool, all seem to acquire a deeper significance when viewed in relation to the events of this day.

"Father, into Your Hands I Commend My Spirit...." (Luke 23:46)

This is no mere "giving up the ghost." It is the Redeemer's dying act, and the ultimate expression of the trinitarian dynamic of love. The Son returns to the Father that Spirit who was sent first to the Virgin, the same Spirit who descended on the Son in the form of a dove at the Baptism in the Jordan (waters again!). In order to die, in order to complete his mission, to conquer death, Jesus must be "parted" from the Spirit. Body, soul, and Spirit must be rent asunder. And so, as Adrienne von Speyr writes in *The Cross:* "Sending the Spirit back to heaven — creating a vacuum as it were — is the preparation for the sacrament of Confirmation, for the risen and ascended Son will send the Spirit of Pentecost upon the believers."

"Lead Us Not into Temptation"

The sixth petition of the Lord's Prayer may also be rendered, "Do not let us give in to temptation" or "save us from the *time of trial.*" Whether the latter reference is to the trials of life, to the "end times," or both is unclear. Certainly, God does not tempt us to sin, but permits temptation as a trial of faith, as a way of strengthening and refining our relationship to him.

It is notable that both the beginning and the end of Jesus's public ministry are marked by an "entering into temptation," a period of inner turmoil and trial; firstly in the desert after his Baptism at the hands of John, and lastly in the garden of Gethsemane after initiating the new Passover with his disciples. Jesus is led into the desert, we are told, by the Holy Spirit; in the garden he advises his disciples to "Watch and pray that you may not enter into temptation" (Matt. 26:41). It is this mystery of temptation to which the Lord's Prayer refers: in Christ's life, temptations prepare him for proclaiming the Gospel through both his public ministry and his humiliating death. All the baptized are living in him, and he in them; they too must experience this trial in order to achieve the final *fiat,* saying to the Father, "If this cannot pass unless I drink it, thy will be done" (Matt. 26:42).

The three temptations that Jesus experiences in the desert summarize all the temptations to which human nature is prone in body, soul, and spirit. That the contest with the Devil is waged at three distinct levels is made clear by the metaphor of height: in Matthew's account we move from ground level ("command that these stones be made bread"), to the "pinnacle of the Temple," to the top of "a very high mountain." Each time, the Devil's temptation would lead to a greater fall. The three temptations are the same that worked on Eve in the Garden of Eden. She took the forbidden fruit because it was "good for food . . . pleasant to the eyes, and . . . to be desired to make one wise" (Gen. 3:6). Our legitimate desire for goodness, beauty, and truth becomes corrupted all too easily into a desire for pleasure, spectacle, and power. Jesus answers all three temptations with humility. They address his human nature; he defeats them by stressing the complete dependence of that nature on the Father's will and grace.

The sacrament of Confirmation strengthens those who receive it to survive the three types of temptation. No one can proclaim the Gospel effectively, or die for it, unless the three temptations are first overcome by and in Jesus himself.[13]

Anointing
Healing Power of the Cross

Anointing, also called the sacrament of the sick, is administered to those who are seriously ill. It is the sacrament of hope, and it contains the promise of the resurrection. To all who receive it, it may be said, "This illness is not to death, but for the glory of God, that the Son of God may be glorified through it" (John 11:4).

Seventh Sign **Raising Lazarus (John 11:1–44)**
and
"I Am the Resurrection and the Life" (John 11:25)

Summoning Lazarus from death is a re-creation of light in darkness, of consciousness out of the night of sleep. "If anyone walks in the day, he does not stumble, because he sees the light of this world. But if anyone walks in the night, he stumbles, because the light is not in him" (John 11:9–10)

After hearing that his friend Lazarus is sick, Jesus significantly delays two days, and then goes to him on the third, only to find after the journey that Lazarus had died and been buried four days earlier. Martha, Lazarus's sister, says to Jesus, "I know that he will rise again in the resurrection, on the last day" (v. 24). Jesus replies, "I am the resurrection and the life; anyone who believes in me, even if he should die will live, and those who live and believe in me shall never die."

In Jesus, the last day (which is also the first) is here already. Yet there is no attempt to play down the tragedy of death. Jesus weeps. His friend has been in the tomb long enough to begin to decompose; returning him to life must involve restoring both his life and his health. To the command, "Lazarus, come forth," the dead man arises. "Did I not tell you that if you believe you will see the glory of God?" (v. 40). Here the connection is made between the resurrection and *seeing* God's glory as though it were light.

First Day **Creating Light**

The seventh sign corresponds to the first day of creation, in which God creates light by his Word: and "God called the light Day, and the darkness he called Night" (Gen. 1:5). Raising

Lazarus points clearly to the coming restoration of all things in the risen Christ, the light of the world. The creation of light out of death is analogous to the first moment of creation, when a new world emerges from darkness. Each sign has signified one aspect of the glory revealed in Christ. Each successive sign has penetrated deeper into the ontological structure of the creation. With the seventh sign, it is the first day that has been reached — the Day that contains in essence all the others. The signs pointed further and further back; the seventh points back before there was light, to the very beginning, to the Trinity itself, about to be revealed through the Passion. "Then I saw a new heaven and a new earth; for the first heaven and the first earth had passed away, and the sea was no more" (Rev. 21:1).

"Today You Will Be with Me in Paradise" (Luke 23:43)

These words are addressed to the dying thief, one of those who are crucified next to Jesus on the hill of Calvary. The thief admits the justice of his own punishment, "for we are receiving the due reward of our deeds; but this man has done nothing wrong." And he asks, "Jesus, remember me when you come into your kingdom" (v. 42). These words evoke the promise of paradise from Jesus.

The thief receives with this promise, writes Adrienne von Speyr in *The Cross,* a "sacrament of dying," which Jesus instituted for his imperfect Church, "a Church into which he accepts everyone who acknowledges him in any way, sinners great and small, and all those in between." The Lord "recognizes in the robber the man for whom he suffers, the man for whom he has opened the way to paradise." "This second Baptism is the sacrament of Anointing, occupying precisely the place which Baptism could have occupied if man had remained in the state of innocence."

The good thief represents all those who suffer without resentment the temporal punishment due for their own sins, turning to the Lord in a spirit of humility and obedience. The Church grants to all of them the same assurance of eternal life, of healing in body and soul.

"Deliver Us from Evil"

The final petition of the Our Father is a prayer of deliverance from the evil one, a prayer for liberation from the power of evil, whether this evil be suffering, sickness, or the death of the soul. Christ died to save us from death — not from dying, but from the power of death, in which we had placed ourselves through sin.

The seventh petition concludes the sequence of the sacraments presented in the Lord's Prayer thus:

> Baptism
>   Marriage
>   Ordination
>   Eucharist
>   Reconciliation
>   Confirmation
> Anointing

The pattern seems to possess its own logic, a variation on the sequence we have been following through John. In both patterns, the Eucharist is central to the series, with Confirmation and Anointing last. In both, Reconciliation is paired with Ordination, forming a kind of central group around which the sacraments of the lay state are wrapped. But the sequence we have been following through John begins with the sacrament of Marriage, pairing this with Anointing and Baptism with Confirmation instead of the other way around, thus:

Marriage

Baptism

Reconciliation

Eucharist

Ordination

Confirmation

Anointing

Both orders make sense. Baptism and Anointing belong together as beginning and end; Marriage and Confirmation are sacraments of adulthood. But Baptism and Confirmation also belong together as stages of initiation, while Marriage and Anointing share the anticipation of the Kingdom.

Summary

Marriage: Coming of the Kingdom
First sign: changing water into wine (John 2:1–11)
"I am the true vine" (John 15:1)
Seventh day: the Sabbath
"Woman, behold your Son" (John 19:25–27)
"Thy kingdom come"

Baptism: Giving of the Name
Second sign: healing the official's son (John 4:46–54)
"I am the way, and the truth, and the life; no one comes to
    the Father, except through me" (John 14:6)
Sixth day: Adam and Eve
"It is accomplished" (John 19:30)
"Our Father, who art in heaven, hallowed be thy name"

Reconciliation: Unveiling of Sin
Third sign: healing the paralyzed man (John 5:1–14)
"I am the door" (John 10:9)
Fifth day: life stirring the waters
"Father, forgive them, for they know not what they do"
    (Luke 23:34)
"Forgive us our trespasses, as we forgive those who trespass
    against us"

Eucharist: Bread of Heaven
Fourth sign: feeding the Five Thousand (John 6:1–15)
"I am the bread of life" (John 6:35–71)
Fourth day: creating the sun
"I thirst" (John 19:28)
"Give us this day our daily bread"

Ordination: Between Heaven and Earth
Fifth sign: walking on the water (John 6:19)
"I am the good shepherd" (John 10:11)
Third day: land in the midst of the waters
"My God, why have you forsaken me?" (Mark 15:34)
"Thy will be done on earth as it is in heaven"

Confirmation: Witness to the Light
Sixth sign: healing the man born blind (John 9:1–40)
"I am the light of the world" (John 9:5)
Second day: creating the sky
"Father, into your hands I commend my Spirit. . . . "
    (Luke 23:46)
"Lead us not into temptation"

Anointing: Healing Power of the Cross
Seventh sign: raising Lazarus (John 11:1–44)
"I am the resurrection and the life" (John 11:25)
First day: creating light
"Today you will be with me in paradise" (Luke 23:43)
"Deliver us from evil"

Notes

1. Mensch, *The Beginning of the Gospel According to St. John*, esp. 92–102. Mensch points out that although John casts both the language and the incidents of his Gospel "in an unmistakable symbolic mode" throughout, this does not imply that what he describes "were not real, historical events." "It does, however, mean that John wishes us to see beyond what took place to the reality which was *signified* by such events" (94).

2. I have adopted the suggestion of reading the days of creation in relation to the seven signs in this (reverse) order from Valentin Tomberg, *Covenant of the Heart*, who also connects each with one of the "I am" sayings. I felt free, however, to depart in many other respects from Tomberg's interpretations, and even from his ordering.

3. The wedding at Cana takes place, in John's carefully constructed chronology, on the third day after he is acknowledged as "King of Israel" by Nathanael (John 1:49). But according to the same Evangelist it is the *seventh* day from Israel's new beginning in the testimony of the Baptist (John 1:19–28).

4. *Catechism of the Catholic Church*, para. 2803.

5. It would (probably rightly!) be regarded as too far-fetched to point out that the man by the pool had been unable to move properly for thirty-eight years, and that the number five may be derived by subtracting three from eight. As already noted number manipulation has a distinguished history in the ancient world, and several studies have been written on the traces of "gematria" and numerical symbolism in Scripture. A striking example of "contemplative mathematics" may be found in von Balthasar, *First Glance at Adrienne von Speyr* (82–85), where he describes her interpretation of the "Fisher's Net" in John 21:11, containing exactly 153 fishes.

6. Here we encounter the paradox of nature and grace. God creates me free, and just as his (uncreated) freedom means I cannot demand grace by right, so my (created) freedom means that God cannot demand my obedience by right: the obligation is one of love. Thus freedom opens in creation a space

for possible sin, for rejecting God's love and breaking obedience. I am free to steal from God, to steal *myself* from God. This is the "debt" that remains unless God "for-gives" it — that is, unless he gives me retrospectively what I took from him while it was still his. And this is what Jesus asks the Father to do. "Forgive them," that is, cancel the obligation of love; do not expect it of them because they are not capable of returning love anymore. Instead, and in return for the love lavished on creation, the Son freely offers to the Father his own perfect self. He does so in a way that bequeaths to us that same sacrifice, so that we who were incapable of returning ourselves freely to the Father can become members of the one who does. He does not leave us to go our own way to self-destruction, but gives his own life to win us back, to inspire us with the very love the Father no longer expects of us. All we must do is to forgive others and ask to be forgiven in our turn.

7. On this point see Ayo, *The Lord's Prayer.*

8. Tomberg considers Ordination as related not to the third day but to the second, and to the sixth sign not the fifth, transposing it in these respects with the sacrament of Confirmation, which I look at next. I suspect that Tomberg was misled by a Gnostic idealization of the Roman Catholic priesthood into assuming its essence to lie in *seeing and witnessing* rather than in *shepherding.*

9. The connection with the third day is so obvious as hardly to need stating. No doubt it would be thought fanciful to suggest a connection between this incident and the washing of feet at the Last Supper, so connected with the ordination of the apostles, or, come to that, with the fact that the apostles are "fishermen," i.e., masters of the deep.

10. As von Speyr writes in *The Gates of Eternal Life,* her book about the sacraments, "The inviolable relation between earth and heaven in the Eucharist is not placed in the hands of the individual believer." It is not any individual believer who consecrates, but only the priest: the mystery is "caused" by the office of the Church, not the faith of the individual. The union of priest and sacrifice that Christ brought about is thus maintained; for although the parish priest is not slain upon the altar, it is not strictly speaking he who offers the sacrifice of the Mass, but Christ in person, uniting heaven and earth through a man he has ordained to bring about the irruption of eternity into time.

11. The distinction between Mary's *fiat* at the beginning of Luke's Gospel and that of Jesus toward the end, on the Mount of Olives, is equivalent to that between the "priesthood of the baptized," as it is called, and the "ministerial priesthood" of the ordained.

12. *Muron,* in Greek, being an oil scented with balm. Summarizing the teaching of the Church Fathers, Jean Daniélou describes Confirmation as a *perfecting:* "It is the putting to use of the new dispositions which result from

the new being created by Baptism. It represents the development of faith into 'gnosis,'" *via* the gifts of the Holy Spirit and the opening of the spiritual senses (*The Bible and the Liturgy*, 124). He tells us that the Holy Spirit's presence in the consecrated *muron* was regarded by Cyril of Jerusalem as akin to the real presence of Christ in the Blessed Sacrament.

13. The sacrament of Confirmation opens up the possibility of regarding the three evangelical counsels not only as a way of perfection for those specially consecrated (the common interpretation), but as the underlying form of *any* adult Christian life. Poverty corresponds to the first temptation, chastity to the second, and obedience to the third, as was suggested earlier.

FIVE

The Structure
of the Covenant

The modern world does not understand the idea of covenants, and it tries to reduce them all to "contracts," that is, to a more superficial and temporary form of agreement.[1] A covenant is a profound union between two or more people, which is why traditionally the establishment of a covenant involved a symbolic shedding of blood (in circumcision, and so forth).[2] Covenants create a bond that is "thicker than water." But the modern world views human beings as individuals, atomic social particles, bound together in temporary molecules that can be split apart and reassembled for the sake of convenience. On this view, the act of self-giving that creates a covenant — the archetype of which Christians recognize in the love of the Trinity — is literally nonsensical. The self must be centered *in* the self, and all its actions in search of fulfillment must be directed toward the self, not to some other person. Altruism is an illusion, a figment of our sociobiological inheritance, serving the reproduction of our genes or masking the dark purposes of the id. (As a result of this attitude to society, the medieval guilds became mere associations of working people, and marriage itself is fast becoming a legal arrangement to facilitate temporary cohabitation.)

If you look at the Ten Commandments in this light, you begin to see how they might form the basis for an entirely different civilization, one founded not on the mythical modern notion of a social contract but on something much deeper: a social covenant with each other and with God. Patrick Riley has argued that the Decalogue is not in the first place a code of ethics at all. The Mosaic Covenant establishes a *family relationship* between God and the people of Israel. God becomes their "father" in a special sense. In fact he also becomes their king. The first three commandments therefore concern the foundations of *political society*, for Israel was a theocracy (a polity ruled by God). The next three commandments may be seen as the foundations of *civil society*, and the remaining four as the foundations of an *economic society*.[3]

The Commandments can be interpreted both as a political code and as the summary of a system of ethics, for the structural rules governing human community are essentially moral and spiritual. In 1998, Pope John Paul II issued an Apostolic Letter called *Dies Domini*, "On Keeping the Lord's Day Holy." Section 13 refers to the Decalogue as "ten words" that represent the very pillars of the moral life inscribed on the human heart, and the basic structure of ethics. (The *Catechism of the Catholic Church* employs them in this way, organizing its description of the moral life under these ten headings.)

The commandments are like the structure of a building. The roof of this building, which shelters and protects it against the wild elements, is *religion*, and it is described in the first three commandments: love God before all else, worship him, and build your society around him. The other seven commandments, the pillars and walls that support the roof, define the space where humanity dwells — they describe the different ways in which we must serve the common good, so we can live together in harmony, to mutual benefit.

It should be noted that the Hebrew Scriptures do not attach numbers to the commandments, except for the clear indication that there are ten of them. This has led to different ways of numbering them in the various traditions. In the Book of Exodus (20:1–11) the text reads: "I am the Lord your God.... You shall not have strange gods before me. You shall not make for yourself a graven image, or any likeness of anything that is in heaven above, or that is in the earth beneath, or that is in the water under the earth; you shall not bow down to them or serve them; for I the Lord your God am a jealous God.... You shall not take the name of the Lord your God in vain.... Remember the sabbath day, to keep it holy." Are these three commandments or four (or indeed five)? This book adopts the standard Catholic approach, which is to regard the prohibition of graven images as belonging to the first commandment. The prohibition is directed not against art (though it has been interpreted as such by iconoclasts at various times in history) but against idol-worship, in order to reinforce the insistence that Israel has only one God. The command not to take the Lord's name in vain is accordingly read as a second rather than a third commandment, and the observance of the sabbath a third.[4]

The first three commandments make possible everything that follows. Without religion, without worship of the divine principle, the only possible result is an ever-greater tendency to close in upon the self. It is true, we have to look out for number one, but the true number one is not myself; it is my Creator. By putting God first — in the first three commandments — we are re-centering the self on something other than itself. In fact, worship (assuming that it is worship of that which deserves to be worshipped!) is the *only way* that the human self can be turned inside out and begin to become unselfish. Love starts with this ability to turn outward, this awakening to the other.

The third commandment — which consecrates the sabbath as a special day of worship and celebration — establishes a "great school of charity, justice and peace" and gives us the "inspiration to change the structures of sin in which individuals, communities and at times entire peoples are entangled" (*Dies Domini,* n. 73). This commandment issues from the first two and prepares us for all that follows — all that makes up the human society that flourishes after the seventh day when God completed his work and waited for man's response. The seventh day is the beginning and end of the human world. It is the day when human history unfolds, and it is day when we will be gathered again at the end, when man is able to rest with God.[5]

The fourth commandment, beseeching us to honor our parents, is the central pillar (the hearth? the doorway?) of our building. It is the respect we give to our parents, our tradition, or our people. It preserves the land, the nation, to which we belong. This is also the way we enter the building and dwell in it: we enter the house from within; we are born and grow up within it. The fifth and sixth commandments describe the sacredness of life and marriage. The seventh and eighth describe the sacredness of property and truth. The final two commandments emphasize the need to be content with what you have: in other words, they tell us to keep our own desires under control so that envy, greed, and resentment do not spring up like weeds in the house and destroy it.

Our Lord Jesus Christ, being both God and man, unites the commandments in his own person: the commandments to love God and to love man. He is at one and the same time the God we must love with all our heart and soul and mind, and the neighbor we must love as ourselves. He also lives the commandments. He is the only one who can live them perfectly. We can live them only by living in him, or by letting him live in us, as the saints

have done. We live in him through belonging to the Church —
through participating in the sacraments.

The Ten Commandments have been understood wrongly as a
set of rules imposed on us by the power of God. In fact they are
not imposed on us from the outside, extrinsically, at all; rather,
they are intrinsic to us. They are the rules by which we are
made. If it were not for them, we would not exist. These rules
are revealed in this particular form, the Decalogue, in order to
reorient or redirect us to our true end, our *telos*. Sin obscured
the natural law of our moral nature from our sight, and the
Decalogue clarifies and confirms what once we would have been
able to see without its help. The order of the commandments
corresponds to the necessary order of this reorientation, the
order of charity. Then at last the new law of the Sermon on
the Mount reveals the pattern of beatitude, the goal of human
nature that is implicit in the commandments, which is also the
form of holiness. This heavenly goal crowns the commandments
and is their reason for existing.

The Sermon on the Mount is a self-portrait of Jesus Christ;
its pattern of holiness is exemplified in Jesus himself. Jesus himself is the meek one, the pure of heart, the one who mourns over
Israel, the one who hungers and thirsts for righteousness. Most
preachers are in some degree hypocritical. They do not practice
what they preach perfectly. Jesus is the exception. As the incarnate Son of God, he is also the *law* incarnate. He represents
the goal of human existence. Hans Urs von Balthasar tells us
that "Christ's concrete existence — his life, suffering, death and
ultimately bodily resurrection — surpasses all other systems of
ethical norms. In the final analysis it is to this norm alone, which
is itself the prototype of perfect obedience to God the Father,
that the moral conduct of Christians has to answer.... In Christ
all have been endowed with the same freedom of children and
heirs, and all are striving towards the same goal."[6]

Grace does not supplant or destroy the natural order, but rather integrates and assumes it. In the case of the natural law codified in the commandments, we can see this very well. Jesus brings a supernatural fulfillment of our natural yearnings for life and friendship and community and peace. Those yearnings are reflected in the Decalogue but cannot be satisfied except in the life that is described in the beatitudes. That life, which is both divine and human, natural and supernatural, is opened to us through the sacraments, which implant within us a receptivity adequate to the infinity of the gift.

There is a close connection between the commandments, the beatitudes, the seven sacraments, and the seven petitions in the Lord's Prayer. We are told in the Sermon on the Mount that the kingdom belongs to the needy, the poor. The virtues that are the treasures of holiness are given only to those who are receptive to them, not to those who are fat and full and contented. People who are conscious of their complete dependence on God are living the Lord's Prayer, asking at all times for their daily bread. They welcome the nourishment that comes to them in the sacraments.

The Ten Commandments

The people of God are constituted by a covenant with God, and the commandments (Exod. 20:2–17 and Deut. 5:6–21) give the rules for living within this covenant, based on God's wisdom and the principles of natural law (see C. S. Lewis, *The Abolition of Man*). The Ten Commandments reveal how to live in a truly human community. They are described in part three of the *Catechism of the Catholic Church*, and summarized in the two commandments of Matthew 22:37–39 (based on Deut. 6:5; Lev. 19:18), as follows.

I. Love the Lord your God with all your heart, and with all your soul, and with all your mind....

Commandment	Expression
1. I am the Lord your God; you shall not have other gods before me.	"Worship the one, true and living God, by Faith, Hope and Love..." *The Baltimore/Penny Catechism*
2. You shall not take the name of the Lord your God in vain.	Reverence, verbal prayer, integrity
3. Remember to keep holy the Lord's day.	Sabbath, jubilee, giving time for worship

II.... and love your neighbor as yourself

4. Honor your father and mother that your days may be long in the land.	Extended family, tradition, tribe, nation, authority, ecology Cf. *CCC*, paras. 1880, 1898
5. You shall not kill [i.e., murder].	Peace, civil order, security, sacredness of life
6. You shall not commit adultery.	Faithful love, chastity, vows
7. You shall not steal.	Property, freedom, justice
8. You shall not bear false witness against your neighbor.	Truth, honesty, integrity, mutual trust, charity, honor
9. You shall not covet your neighbor's wife	Respect, modesty, purity of heart
10. You shall not covet your neighbor's goods	Detachment, temperance, generosity

The *Ten Commandments* are summarized in the *two great commandments*. But the two commandments, in turn, are summarized by Jesus in what he calls the **new commandment**: "Love one another, *as I have loved you*" (John 13:34; 15:9–17).

The Beatitudes and the Our Father *or* How to Obey the Commandments

"*The Commandments are linked to a promise.* In the Old Covenant the object of this promise was the possession of a land where the people would live in freedom and in accordance with righteousness (cf. Deut. 6:20–25). In the New Covenant the object of the promise is the kingdom of heaven, as Jesus declares at the beginning of the 'Sermon on the Mount' — a sermon which contains the fullest and most complete form of the New Law, clearly linked to the Decalogue entrusted by God to Moses on Mount Sinai" (John Paul II, *Veritatis Splendor* 12). "*Jesus brings God's commandments to fulfillment*, particularly the commandment of love of neighbor, *by interiorizing their demands and by bringing out their fullest meaning.* . . . Jesus shows that the commandments must not be understood as a minimum limit not to be gone beyond, but rather as a path involving a moral and spiritual journey towards perfection [i.e., holiness], at the heart of which is love" (*Veritatis Splendor* 15). Saint Augustine tells us how to travel this spiritual path by connecting each beatitude with a petition from the Our Father (Matt. 6:9–15) as shown below. I have introduced each with one of the seven commandments that particularly concern the love of neighbor, adding a few words of commentary to bring out the relevance as best I can.[7]

Commandment	Beatitude	Petition
Fourth: We have inherited everything from others; honor the source!	Blessed are the poor in spirit, for the kingdom of heaven is theirs.	*Hallowed be thy name.*
Fifth: To avoid killing, you must give life.	Blessed are the meek, for they shall inherit the earth.	*Thy kingdom come.*
Sixth: To avoid adultery, you must be faithful until death.	Blessed are those who mourn, for they shall be comforted.	*Thy will be done on earth as in heaven.*
Seventh: To avoid stealing, you must learn to desire only what belongs to you.	Blessed are those who hunger and thirst for justice, for they shall be satisfied.	*Give us this day our daily bread.*
Eighth: To vindicate others, you must forgive them.	Blessed are the merciful, for they shall obtain mercy.	*Forgive us our debts, as we forgive others.*
Ninth: To be free of lust, you must purify your imagination.	Blessed are the pure in heart, for they shall see God.	*Lead us not into temptation.*
Tenth: To overcome greed and ambition, you must make peace with those around you.	Blessed are the peace-makers, for they shall be called the children of God.	*But deliver us from evil.*

And blessed are those who suffer persecution for my sake....
The final beatitude refers to the likely fate of those who try to live the other seven!

The Gifts of the Holy Spirit and Beatitudes

If each petition or request contained in the Our Father has at its heart a prayer for precisely that inward and spiritual gift of grace that we need to live one of the beatitudes (to love each other as Jesus loves us), and thus the commandments, it is not too surprising to find that each petition also corresponds to one of the traditional gifts of the Holy Spirit, as listed by the Prophet Isaiah (11:1–2) and recalled by the Christian Church each year at Pentecost. Summarized below, this teaching is drawn from Saint Augustine, who reverses the more familiar order of the gifts so as to begin the sequence with Fear of the Lord and end with Wisdom.

Petition	Gift	Beatitude
Hallowed be thy name.	Fear of the Lord	Blessed are the poor in spirit. *Respect for the divine name is the beginning of wisdom.*
Thy kingdom come.	Piety	Blessed are the meek [humble]. *Humility brings the kingdom down to the earth.*
Thy will be done on earth as it is in heaven.	Knowledge	Blessed are those who mourn. *This refers to the gift of tears that flows from knowledge.*
Give us this day our daily bread.	Fortitude	Blessed are those who hunger and thirst for justice. *They are sustained by courage.*
Forgive us our debts, as we forgive others.	Counsel	Blessed are the merciful. *God counsels us to forgive in order to be forgiven.*
Lead us not into temptation.	Understanding	Blessed are the pure in heart. *To understand is to see God with the eyes of faith.*
But deliver us from evil.	Wisdom	Blessed are the peacemakers. *Eternal peace lies only in the wisdom of God.*

Pinckaers writes that the correlation of the beatitudes to the gifts enables us to "reconcile morality with the desire for happiness."[8] It "leads us to abandon the separation between morality and spirituality (ascetical and mystical), in order to give morality a truly spiritual dimension, as 'life in the Spirit.' It is through the gifts, in fact, that the Holy Spirit inspires Christian life, giving believers interior light and impulse."

He adds: "Today we realize more and more the need for prayer in theological reflection. Under the influence of rationalism, we have too long believed that theology was a work of pure reason and prayer a matter of emotion. We have forgotten that the theologian cannot acquire an experiential, accurate understanding of what he teaches without the light of grace and therefore of prayer, without his share in the gifts of wisdom, understanding, knowledge, and counsel."

The Commandments, Sacraments, and Lord's Prayer

Each of the Church's sacraments is a visible symbol of the invisible divine grace that it transmits. That is, each sacrament mediates the divine energies that make it possible for us to obey the moral law, by uniting us in a shared life or communion with the one who lived that law perfectly, Jesus Christ. Thus each of the sacraments can be understood as an answer to one of the petitions of the Lord's Prayer (also called the Our Father, or in Latin *Paternoster*), as follows below.

Finally, each sacrament with its corresponding petition can be associated with one of the seven commandments pertaining directly to the love of neighbor, as the brief commentary suggests.

Commandment	Sacrament	Petition (and commentary)
Fourth	Baptism	**Hallowed be thy name.** One is adopted into the family of God when given a Christian name.
Fifth	Marriage	**Thy kingdom come.** Marriage gives life to the children who will populate the kingdom of God.
Sixth	Ordination	**Thy will be done on earth as it is in heaven.** The priest follows Christ in doing the Father's will, joining earth to heaven.
Seventh	Eucharist	**Give us this day our daily bread.** Holy Communion gives us bread from heaven, filling us with every good thing.[9]
Eighth	Reconciliation	**Forgive us our trespasses [debts], as we forgive others.** God's forgiveness is conditional on our reconciliation with others.
Ninth	Confirmation	**Lead us not into temptation.** The sacrament strengthens us against temptation.
Tenth	Anointing	**Deliver us from evil.** The sacrament of the sick prepares us to meet death, detaches us from worldly things, and helps to reconcile us with our neighbor.

The Sacraments and the Seven Last Words

Adrienne von Speyr's commentaries on Scripture were recorded and published by Hans Urs von Balthasar. Her little book *The Cross: Word and Sacrament,* described in the first chapter and summarized below, focuses on Jesus's seven last words.

The Church is no mere institution. She is the living extension of the Incarnation. Her existence is implicit in the Redeemer's every action. So von Speyr writes: "If the Lord's words are all of a piece with his life, and if he surrenders his life on the Cross for his Church, it follows that the Lord's words from the Cross are closely knit to, parallel to, the sacraments, those vessels of the life of divine grace which overflows from the Cross into the Church."

As we have seen, this vision of faith is in accord with that of the Fathers and saints. "What our great Redeemer did visibly has passed over into the sacraments," writes Saint Leo the Great (Serm. LXXIV, *De Ascens.*). Of course, the Gospels record several distinct moments of institution ("Go baptize...," "Do this in memory of me...."), but these are not isolated acts of will. The sacraments are founded on the Lord's entire life, a life of supreme inner consistency; the echoes of their institution can be heard everywhere.

Sacrament	Last Words	Note from von Speyr's commentary
Reconciliation	*Father, forgive them* (Luke 23:34).	Our Lord "knows that they cannot be held fully responsible, and the conclusion he draws is this: *he* will bear the responsibility *himself.*"
Anointing	*Today you will be with me in paradise* (Luke 23:43).	This "second Baptism" occupies "the place which Baptism could have occupied if man had remained in the state of ignorance."
Marriage	*Woman, behold your Son...behold your Mother* (John 19:25–27).	"This couple [Mary and John] is created by the Lord's word from the Cross. In some way they thus become an original couple like Adam and Eve."

Sacrament	Last Words	Note from von Speyr's commentary
Ordination	*My God, why have you forsaken me?* (Mark 15:34).	Jesus finds us even in the depths of our despair, "bearing *in advance* all that will happen to…those who were willing to dedicate themselves" and renounce human companionship.
Eucharist	*I thirst* (John 19:28).	"Because he emptied himself until his whole self was nothing but a burning void, we possess him as Eucharist."
Baptism	*It is accomplished* (John 19:30).	"What seems to be the end to the dying man on the Cross is in fact the opening of his life to all times in the Church."
Confirmation	*Father, into your hands I commend my spirit* (Luke 23:46).	In order to complete his mission, Jesus must be parted from the Spirit. "But the risen and ascended Son will send the Spirit of Pentecost upon the believers."

The Sacraments in Spiritual Warfare

Despite the militaristic tone of this heading, it refers to the long-standing use among the great spiritual writers of warfare as a metaphor to describe the inner struggle for purity and integrity. In his summary of the faith called *Breviloquium*, Saint Bonaventure explains the distinct function of each sacrament in this continual struggle for personal sanctification. Each heals us of a specific type of sin or weakness, restores in us a particular power or virtue, and preserves us in an appropriate spiritual state.[10]

Sacrament	Expels	Restores	Preserves
Baptism	Original sin	Faith	Motivates those entering battle
Reconciliation	Mortal sin	Justice	Renews the injured or defeated
Anointing	Venial sin	Fortitude	Strengthens those leaving battle
Ordination	Ignorance	Prudence	Revives spiritual life
Eucharist	Malice	Charity	Revitalizes those recuperating
Confirmation	Weakness	Hope	Fortifies the warrior
Marriage	Lust	Temperance	Bestows natural life and recruits

Seven Words and Seven Sins

Archbishop Fulton J. Sheen, a popular broadcaster and spiritual writer of the twentieth century, correlates Jesus's seven last words from the Cross with the seven capital or deadly sins of Catholic tradition in his book *The Seven Capital Sins*. I have added a further layer to this by adding the seven sacraments, using the schema derived from Adrienne von Speyr.

Last Word	Sin	Sacrament
"Father, forgive them"	Anger	Reconciliation
"Today you will be with me in paradise"	Envy	Anointing
"Woman, behold your Son"	Lust	Marriage
"My God, why have you forsaken me?"	Pride	Ordination
"I thirst"	Gluttony	Eucharist
"It is accomplished"	Sloth	Baptism
"Into your hands I commend my spirit"	Covetousness	Confirmation

The Seven Churches

The Book of Revelation includes at least seven sets of seven: seven churches (2:1–3:22), seven seals (6:1–8:1), seven trumpets (8:2–11:19), seven mysterious figures (12:1–13:18), seven bowls (15:1–16:21), seven dooms (17:1–20:15), and seven "new things" (21:1–22:21). Now to correlate each of these sets with the seven sacraments might be said to be an obvious case of carrying things a bit too far. In the case of the seven churches, however, correspondences do seem to be fairly easy to read into the text. Why might this be? Perhaps each symbolic church corresponds to the universal Church viewed, as it were, through the lens of one of the sacraments. In order to make this more evident, I have linked each sacrament to one of the churches, and in each heading I have placed a phrase that picks out a theme relevant to the sacrament from the passage below. Each passage from Revelation can then be read as a meditation on the appropriate sacrament.

1. **Baptism — Return to paradise**

   "To the angel of the Church in Ephesus write. . . . Remember then from what you have fallen, repent and do the works you did at first. . . . To him who conquers I will grant to eat of the tree of life, which is in the Paradise of God" (Rev. 2:1–7).

2. **Confirmation — Strengthening for the test**

   "To the angel of the Church in Smyrna write. . . . Do not fear what you are about to suffer. Behold, the devil is about to throw some of you into prison, that you may be tested. . . . Be faithful unto death, and I will give you the crown of life" (Rev. 2:8–11).

3. **Eucharist — Bread from heaven**

   "To the angel of the church in Pergamum write. . . . To him who conquers I will give some of the hidden manna, and I will give him a white stone, with a name written on the stone which no one knows except him who receives it" (Rev. 2:12–17).

4. **Marriage — Loving faithfulness**

   "To the angel of the church in Thyatira write. . . . I know your works, your love and faith and service and patient endurance, and that your latter works exceed the first. But I have this against you, that you tolerate the woman Jezebel. . . . Behold, I will throw

her on a sickbed, and those who commit adultery with her I will throw into a great tribulation.... But to the rest of you ... hold fast to what you have, until I come. He who conquers and who keeps my words until the end, I will give him authority over the nations ... and I will give him the morning star" (Rev. 2:18–29).

5. Anointing — Strengthening at the point of death

"To the angel of the church in Sardis write.... Awake, and strengthen what remains and is on the point of death, for I have not found your works perfect in the sight of my God.... He who conquers shall be clad thus in white garments, and I will not blot his name out of the book of life" (Rev. 3:1–6).

6. Ordination — Power of the keys

"To the angel of the church in Philadelphia write: The words of the Holy One, the true one, who has the key of David, who opens and no one shall shut, who shuts and no one opens.... He who conquers, I will make him a pillar in the temple of my God" (Rev. 3:7–13).

7. Reconciliation — Penance

"To the angel of the church of Laodicea write.... I counsel you to buy from me gold refined by fire, that you may be rich ... and white garments ... and salve to anoint your eyes.... Those whom I love, I reprove and chasten; so be zealous and repent. Behold, I stand at the door and knock" (Rev. 3:14–22).

The Wheel of Sevens

Not every pattern of seven in Scripture or tradition can be forced into a scheme that relates it to the seven sacraments. The magic number's attraction has always been immense, and lists of seven are commonplace. Their most frequent use is simply as a mnemonic device, aiding recall of information. In the twelfth century, Hugh of Saint Victor wrote a book on the "septenaries" (*De quinque septens seu septenariis*), later drawn in the form of a Wheel of Sevens. In 1310 the Psalter of Robert de Lisle (currently in the British Library), apparently based on Hugh's work, linked each of the petitions of the Lord's Prayer to: sacraments, gifts of the Holy Spirit, the spiritual weapons of the virtues, the corporeal and spiritual works of mercy, and the capital virtues and vices. It does so in a way that sometimes differs from the present book: a salutary warning that tradition is by no means uniform. The following table lays out the ten sets of correlations we have explored above for ease of reference. (The order is dictated here by the petitions in the Our Father. For reasons of space, each is identified by a key word only.)

Sacrament *Sign*	*Petition* *Last Word*	*Gift* *I Am*	*Beatitude* *Commandment*	*Virtue* *Day of Creation*
Baptism	Hallowed be	Fear	Poor	Faith
Second	Accomplished	The way	Fourth	Sixth
Marriage	Kingdom	Piety	Meek	Temperance
First	Behold	Vine	Fifth	Seventh
Ordination	Thy will	Knowledge	Mourn	Prudence
Fifth	Forsaken	Shepherd	Sixth	Third
Eucharist	Bread	Fortitude	Hunger	Love
Fourth	Thirst	Bread	Seventh	Fourth
Reconciliation	Forgive	Counsel	Merciful	Justice
Third	Forgive	Door	Eighth	Fifth
Confirmation	Temptation	Understanding	Pure	Hope
Sixth	Spirit	Light	Ninth	Second
Anointing	Deliver	Wisdom	Peacemakers	Fortitude
Seventh	Today	Resurrection	Tenth	First

Notes

1. Parts of the present chapter are based on chapters 5 and 11 in Caldecott, *Catholic Social Teaching.*

2. On all this, see Hahn, *A Father Who Keeps His Promises* and *First Comes Love.*

3. Riley, *Civilizing Sex.*

4. In order to keep the number of commandments to exactly ten (the "ten words" of Exod. 34:28 and Deut. 4:13; 10:4), this difference at the beginning has consequences later on in the sequence. The Exodus text finishes as follows: "You shall not covet your neighbor's house; you shall not covet your neigbor's wife, or his manservant or his maidservant, or his ox, or his ass, or anything that is your neighbor's." Catholics see here two commandments, not one: against the coveting of another's wife, and of his property. The alternative wording of the Decalogue at Deuteronomy 5:21 gives a basis for this distinction.

5. See Pieper, *Leisure, The Basis of Culture.*

6. Ratzinger, Schurmann, Balthasar, *Principles of Christian Morality,* 82.

7. See the *Catechism (CCC)* on the New Law, paras. 1965–86. For the Sermon on the Mount see Matt. 5:1–12. Read Pinckaers, *The Sources of Christian Ethics* (134–67), for a full exposition of Augustine's and Aquinas's beautiful interpretation of the Sermon on the Mount in relation to the petitions of the Our Father and the gifts of the Holy Spirit (see below).

8. Pinckaers, *The Sources of Christian Ethics* (151–59).

9. "The Church cherishes the truth of this Bread at the heart of its life of solidarity with and preferential option for the world's poor" (Michael Gaudoin-Parker, *Heart in Pilgrimage,* 115). See also the same author's *Hymn of Freedom: Celebrating and Living the Eucharist.* The word *epiousios* means more than "daily." Saint Jerome translated it (in Matthew) as "supersubstantial." It refers both to whatever we need to sustain life and also to that which sustains us for eternal life: the bread of life himself (John 6:41).

10. This summary is based on Miller, *Marriage,* 65.

SIX

The Sacraments and the Days of Creation

We have been looking mainly at the sevenfold mystery of the sacraments of the new covenant. I approached this mystery from several different angles. Now I want to reflect more deeply on the sevenfold mystery that dominated the old covenant (the Hebrew Scriptures or Old Testament), namely the mystery of creation in seven days.

Despite the best efforts of modern exegetes to demythologize and deconstruct the Word of God (and the best efforts of biblical fundamentalists to reduce it to absurdity), Holy Scripture stands aloof amidst the wreckage of our civilization, as enigmatic as the Egyptian sphinx among the desert sands. Yet the Hebrew and Christian scriptures are much more than the monument of some distant, half-forgotten culture. They possess an inexhaustible vitality, and in them a world of meaning may still be discovered by the seeker who explores them in the correct spirit and with the right precautions.

In the opening chapters of its first (though not chronologically earliest) book, the Bible clearly intends to convey the fact that God created and so ordered the world that he remains its supreme ruler and that man (male and female) has a special and in some ways central role within it. How much else the

Bible intends to convey is a matter for dispute. Modern exegetes — professional interpreters of biblical text — constantly on the defensive against science, tend to minimize the range of possible meanings. A whole world of allegorical and mystical commentaries, both Jewish and Christian, has been swept away in recent times, as scholarly attention focused primarily on the historical and literary construction of the text itself (the "Yahwist" versus the "priestly" author and so on). The literal meaning has been reduced to the meaning that modern scholars believe its original authors *must have consciously intended*, taking into account the nature of their civilization and the appropriate literary genre.

In fact, the approach of modern scholarship is almost entirely speculative, since the history of the texts and the mentality of their authors remain fundamentally inaccessible to us. Furthermore, a fashionable hermeneutics of suspicion has tended to divorce the scholarly from the spiritual, typological, or devotional reading of the texts, undermining the confidence with which Christian believers meditate on the Word of God. Scripture is used in the Church's liturgy and formal prayers, where this kind of reading is more appropriate, but homilies or sermons tend to confine themselves to the most basic moral or dogmatic points to be drawn from the texts. In private *lectio divina* (spiritual reading as practiced in religious orders and by those influenced by them) prayerful openness to the Spirit of God who is present in the biblical Word is encouraged, but the fear of reading too much into the text drives such reflections into a corner. One may feel the heart has been uplifted and stirred to prayer, but little true intellectual engagement has taken place. After all, most of us are conscious of lacking the most rudimentary professional or academic qualifications for such engagement.

Without wishing to call the importance of modern biblical scholarship into question, I would question whether we need always to be quite so concerned about the editorial and authorial history of the texts. To adopt a hermeneutics of trust rather than of suspicion and adopt a principle of *maximum possible meaning* is not necessarily to be naïve or pre-critical. What the literary archaeologists can tell us about the text's construction or the (conscious) intentions of the various human authors is of interest, but surely of secondary interest. The meaning of each verse of the Bible, if read in the context of the whole canon, is not limited to the meaning that was intended when that text was originally composed: its meaning is potentially inexhaustible. Catholics are naturally concerned to rule out individual interpretations that may be inconsistent with Church doctrine (for it is the Church which gave us the Bible in the first place by selecting the canon) or with other meanings and matters of fact already established, but this leaves considerable scope for interpretation, not to mention playful if devout exploration. In this respect, I have tried in this book to stay within the limits of legitimate speculation, however idiosyncratic my interpretations may appear.

Now the account of creation in seven days, which we find in the first chapter of Genesis, does not appear to match very closely the order of events we have been led to expect by modern science. Light and plants are created before the sun and moon, for example, and fishes before land animals. Christian fundamentalists and so-called creation scientists have had a wonderful time attempting to fit the scientific account to the revealed one or vice versa (usually the former). But what these fundamentalists do not seem to understand is that Genesis is written in a mythic or *mythopoeic* genre. It was not intended to convey what we today would call a historical order of events. The underlying structure of the days is not chronological but metaphysical, as the following meditation suggests.

The First Account of Creation

The first three days of creation according to the Genesis account proceed by way of differentiation: light from dark, upper from lower waters, land from sea. In the very beginning there is a distinction between the spirit or breath of God (*ruach*) and the formless deep (*tohu wabohu*), which we may consider the pure potentiality to receive form, entirely dependent on God's capacity to give.

Day One

> In the beginning God created the heavens and the earth. The earth was without form and void, and darkness was upon the face of the deep; and the Spirit of God was moving over the face of the waters. And God said, "Let there be light"; and there was light. And God saw that the light was good; and God separated the light from the darkness. God called the light Day, and the darkness he called Night. And there was evening and there was morning, one day.

The work of the first day separates essence from existence, thus giving rise to created being. God is the supremely simple one, whose essence and existence are identical, and all created beings (even angels) differ from him in this single vital respect.[1]

Anointing. This sacrament prepares us for death. In Christ's re-making of the world, signified and effected by the mysteries of the Church, the last sacrament is equivalent to the first day of creation. In facing death or serious illness, we are facing the ultimate darkness, out of which only God has the power to bring light.

Day Two

> And God said, "Let there be a firmament in the midst of the waters, and let it separate the waters from the waters." And God made the firmament and separated the waters which were under the firmament from the waters which were above the firmament. And it was so. And God called the firmament Heaven. And there was evening and there was morning, a second day.

The second day establishes the vertical differentiation of created being: the upper and lower waters, with a firmament separating or mediating between them.

Confirmation. On the second day God establishes a space between the upper and lower waters — a space into which the Holy Spirit may descend, as he does on Pentecost, bringing with him the seven gifts.

Day Three

> And God said, "Let the waters under the heavens be gathered together into one place, and let the dry land appear." And it was so. God called the dry land Earth, and the waters that were gathered together he called Seas. And God saw that it was good. And God said, "Let the earth put forth vegetation, plants yielding seed, and fruit trees bearing fruit in which is their seed, each according to its kind, upon the earth." And it was so. The earth brought forth vegetation, plants yielding seed according to their own kinds, and trees bearing fruit in which is their seed, each according to its kind. And God saw that it was good. And there was evening and there was morning, a third day.

The third day establishes the horizontal differentiation of the states or planes of existence that were achieved on the second day; in other words, dry land was created in the midst of the waters, with plants (their sap flowing, and their leaves unfolding from a central stem in a horizontal plane) mediating between land and water, earth and sky. This day plants the seed principles (*logoi* or "seminal reasons") of all things that are later to develop in time.

Ordination. The sacrament of Holy Orders establishes the man who receives it in the position of mediator between heaven and earth; spiritually speaking, the priest is called to be solid land in the midst of the waters. The priest also represents God as the Father; that is, as the one who makes creation fertile, implanting seeds within it.

Day Four

Like the first set of three days, each of the second set of three days also involves an act of creation by separation or polarization — in this case sun and moon, birds and fishes, animals and man.

> *And God said, "Let there be lights in the firmament of the heavens to separate the day from the night; and let them be for signs and for seasons and for days and years, and let them be lights in the firmament of the heavens to give light upon the earth." And it was so. And God made the two great lights, the greater light to rule the day, and the lesser light to rule the night; he made the stars also. And God set them in the firmament of the heavens to give light upon the earth, to rule over the day and over the night, and to separate the light from the darkness. And God saw that it was good. And there was evening and there was morning, a fourth day.*

In a symbolic cosmos, the sun, moon, and stars of the fourth day are not merely astronomical bodies in the modern sense; they represent the angelic beings whose home is the upper waters. Creating these heavenly bodies marks the first stage in animating a cosmos established on multiple planes.

Eucharist. The Eucharist is the sun among the sacraments, the actual presence of Christ in the cosmos, the "true light that enlightens every man" (John 1:9), the center of the new creation.

Day Five

And God said, "Let the waters bring forth swarms of living creatures, and let birds fly above the earth across the firmament of the heavens." So God created the great sea monsters and every living creature that moves, with which the waters swarm, according to their kinds, and every winged bird according to its kind. And God saw that it was good. And God blessed them, saying, "Be fruitful and multiply and fill the waters in the seas, and let birds multiply on the earth." And there was evening and there was morning, a fifth day.

The fifth day manifests the various forms of life that move up and down in the air and sea (that is, along the vertical axis established on the second day).

Reconciliation. The mystery of confession and absolution has to do with life below and above the land; that is, with sub-conscious and superconscious forces in man that are brought into harmony by the sacrament and by the priest's mediation of divine grace.

Day Six

And God said, "Let the earth bring forth living creatures according to their kinds: cattle and creeping things and beasts of the earth according to their kinds." And it was so. And God made the beasts of the earth according to their kinds and the cattle according to their kinds, and everything that creeps upon the ground according to its kind. And God saw that it was good. Then God said, "Let us make man in our image, after our likeness; and let them have dominion over the fish of the sea, and over the birds of the air, and over the cattle, and over all the earth, and over every creeping thing that creeps upon the earth." So God created man in his own image, in the image of God he created him; male and female he created them. And God blessed them, and God said to them, "Be fruitful and multiply, and fill the earth and subdue it; and have dominion over the fish of the sea and over the birds of the air and over every living thing that moves upon the earth." And God said, "Behold, I have given you every plant yielding seed which is upon the face of all the earth, and every tree with seed in its fruit; you shall have them for food. And to every beast of the earth, and to every bird of the air, and to everything that creeps on the earth, everything that has the breath of life, I have given every green plant for food." And it was so. And God saw everything that he had made, and behold, it was very good. And there was evening and there was morning, a sixth day.

The beasts created on the sixth day are those which move across the horizontal plane established on the third day.

Baptism. Man is re-established in God's image. He is granted dominion over the plane of earthly existence by virtue of the sacrament of Baptism, which implants the divine life within him.

Day Seven

Thus the heavens and the earth were finished, and all the host of them. And on the seventh day God finished his work which he had done, and he rested on the seventh day from all his work which he had done. So God blessed the seventh day and hallowed it, because on it God rested from all his work which he had done in creation.

On the seventh day the various pairs and polarities achieve their state of balance, one with another. A process of separation has established a new harmony, a new unity.

Marriage. The eschatological sacrament derives its mystery from the union of Christ and his Church, and from unity of the human and divine natures in Christ. The communion of two in one flesh fulfills the divine plan for creation.

The Metaphysics of Genesis

The relationships between the seven days can be represented in a diagram like this:

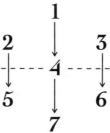

An alternative tradition that is sometimes traced to the Pseudo-Clementine Homilies represents the six days by the six directions of space, with the seventh as the space in the center to which they return. Here the days are paired not vertically, but according to each of the three dimensions: up-down, left-right, and back-front. The equivalent arrangement in two dimensions involves a wheel with six spokes joined in the middle by a central axis:

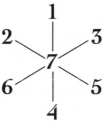

Yet a third version would employ the seven-branched candelabrum or *menorah* (Exod. 25:31–40). Here the days of creation could be assigned to the candles in the following order around 7 in the center: 1, 2, 3, 7, 6, 5, 4.

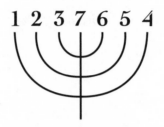

Although these diagrams differ, the relationships are the same in each: days 1 and 4 are paired together (on opposite sides of 7), as are 2 and 5, and 3 and 6. The world of light and dark is populated with the celestial rulers of day and night (1 and 4), the firmament and waters are populated with birds and fishes (2 and 5), and the dry land is populated with animals and man (3 and 6).

It may be instructive to draw upon the rich tradition of Jewish mystical and metaphysical interpretation of Genesis as preserved and elaborated in the medieval Kabbalah. Central to this tradition are the ten *Sefiroth,* or cosmic structural principles (archetypes) seen by the Jewish kabbalists as underlying the Decalogue. These Sefiroth are the aspects or "names" of the one God through which he creates the world we know, and are often depicted in the form of a diagram known as the Tree of the Sefiroth. Some authors identify this with the tree of life, as distinct from the tree of the knowledge of good and evil, spoken of in the second and third chapters of Genesis, and also to the first set of tablets of the law that Moses produced on Sinai. Moses supposedly destroyed these tablets when he saw that the people had been worshipping a golden calf and were therefore unworthy of God's direct revelation (Exod. 32:15–16, 19; 34:1–28). These first tablets "were the light and doctrine of the Messiah, the outpouring of universal deliverance, the source of eternal life on earth."[2] Out of consideration for human weakness, the second set of tablets that Moses delivered to the people concealed the revelation of God's Wisdom (*Hokhmah*) behind the curtain of his Intelligence (*Binah*). These tablets contained the Ten Commandments: positive and negative precepts, giving both life and death.

Without necessarily embracing such speculations, or indeed the Kabbalah itself, we may find the Tree of the Sefiroth helpful in our meditations on Genesis, giving it a Christian interpretation. The Sefiroth are usually listed in the following order.

1. *Kether* (Crown)
2. *Hokhmah* (Wisdom)
3. *Binah* (Understanding)
4. *Chesed* (Mercy)
5. *Geburah* (Severity)
6. *Tiphareth* (Beauty)
7. *Netzach* (Victory)
8. *Hod* (Glory)
9. *Yesod* (Foundation)
10. *Malkuth* (Kingdom)

The upper part of the Tree consists of the three Sefiroth of Emanation, which together represent the "great face" of God. *Kether* is God as he is in himself, *Hokhmah* the divine Wisdom that is the first radiation of the divine, and *Binah* the mirror that receives and transmits this radiation. These three are to be understood as one, Wisdom and Understanding being the active (masculine) and receptive (feminine) aspects of divine self-knowledge (*Kether*).

It is the lower part of the Tree, containing the seven Sefiroth of Construction, corresponding to the days of creation in Genesis, with which we will be concerned here. These seven Sefiroth are arranged in the traditional diagram in three columns:

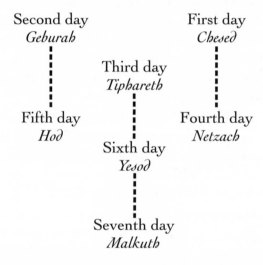

This pattern of three columns yields the same pairs of days as our previous diagrams, if read from top to bottom: 1 and 4, 2 and 5, 3 and 6, with 7 at the base.

But what does all this tell us about the sacraments?

Chesed is the first manifestation of the triune God within the necessary limitations of a cosmos. This tells us that the first creative act is an act of love, imparting Grace, divine Mercy. It corresponds to the creation of light on the first day. It is associated with the prayer "Deliver us from evil" and is concerned with the final deliverance from mortality and hell — as the good thief was assured of his salvation from the Cross. Jesus's last act on earth, like God's act of creation, is an act of love, a manifestation of divine Mercy. The second manifestation of God in the series of Sefiroth is inseparable from and complementary to the first: this is *Geburah* or Severity, Rigor (also known as *Din* or Judgment), which separates God from all that is not divine. It recalls the vertical separation of waters that takes place on the second day. *Geburah* illuminates the nature of the second sacrament, Confirmation, which is concerned on the one hand with the distance between earth and heaven — traversed by the Holy Spirit as he descends at Pentecost to confirm the Apostles in their faith — and on the other with the ability of the Christian to make right judgment, based on the understanding rooted in a pure heart.

The more we examine the details of the Tree and the relationships and natures of the various Sefiroth, the more we find our intuitions about the sacraments and their interrelationship confirmed and strengthened by this system of meditation.

The third Sefirah of Construction, *Tiphareth* or Beauty, occupies a middle or mediating position in the Tree. A dazzling balance of Rigor and Mercy, *Tiphareth* is sometimes referred to as the "son." It represents for kabbalists the act of redemption and for Christians it might just as well represent the sacrament of Ordination, since the Christian priest takes the place of the Redeemer. The third day is that on which the dry land is established in the midst of the waters, and this image recalls the vital role of Ordination in giving the Church solid ground on which to stand: the Christian stands on the rock of Peter. *Tiphareth* in turn gives rise to the fourth Sefirah of Construction, *Netzach* (Victory, or the Eucharist in our table of correlations). It is paired with the Sefirah that stands below it in the central column, *Yesod* (Foundation), equivalent to the creation of man on the sixth day and to Baptism, the latter being the completion of the mediator's work, according to Jesus's last word, "It is accomplished."

Netzach is the fruit of the outpouring of divine Grace (*Chesed*), which stands vertically above it, just as the Eucharist contains all grace because it contains Christ. The consecration of the Eucharist by the priest is suggested by the fact that *Netzach* emanates from *Tiphareth*. However, the Sefirah representing the completion of God's creative work on the sixth day is the fruit of *Netzach* and *Hod* (Glory) together — the latter representing the sacrament of Reconciliation. In other words, the Eucharist brings about the reconciliation (forgiveness) of man in order to bear fruit in the creation of a new humanity.

The Sefirah at the base of the central column, *Malkuth* (Kingdom), corresponding to God's rest on the seventh day and to the sacrament of Marriage, embodies the final descent of God's lifegiving energies into the world, and the union of masculine and feminine. It is called Kingdom and also *Shekinah* because it represents God's immanence, his indwelling of the creation of which he is the king. In Christian terms, this is the great mystery (Eph. 5:32) of Christ and the Church, the divine marriage of God and man.

The Second Account of Creation

The events described in Genesis occur in a world intermediate between time and eternity, among the archetypes of created things. This is the world of God's imagination, a world "inside" history. The Fall narrative does not describe events that happened exclusively in the past and are now over. It is the account of a catastrophe that is *still happening.* The Fall is still going on — "up there," we might say, or "in here." This gives the Genesis accounts an immediate relevance and applicability to each of us, and that is how the Church Fathers always insisted on reading them.

There are two distinct accounts of the creation in Genesis. The first (Gen. 1:1–2:3), the recitation of the seven days, is the one that I have just presented in some detail. It describes the creation of light and even of living plants as preceding that of the sun, while man appears at the end, as a kind of culmination of the process, after which God rests. But the second account (Gen. 2:4–25) is rather different. Man comes first, followed by plants, animals, and finally woman. Both accounts, on our hypothesis, describe the same archetypal creation. The first, however, describes it from an objective, angelic, or divine point of view; that is, from the point of view of the ontological center. It is an obviously metaphysical account, even if the metaphysics is embodied in poetry; our brief and highly condensed survey of the Sefiroth attempted to demonstrate that. As Pope John Paul II says in *The Theology of the Body:* "The first account of man's creation...conceals within itself a powerful metaphysical content."[3] The second account of creation in the Book of Genesis gives a more human-centered view. Its angle, as the Pope says, is "subjective," by which he means that it is concerned more with human self-knowledge. The component parts of the world are set out in relation to man, as though for his sake: the world reveals its human meaning. Man is formed from the earth; the plants are raised up to create a garden for him to dwell in; the animals and birds are formed to give him companionship and help. The day ends with a night, or at least a sleep, in which woman is drawn out of man.

The focus of the second account is primarily, therefore, on what takes place on the sixth day of creation — which we may call the day of the animals. But here too, below the surface of the text, which takes the form of a poetic or mythological narrative, a metaphysical sap is flowing. What we can discern here is of particular relevance to the sacramental mysteries of Baptism and Marriage.

Baptism. We have already noted that the sixth day is particularly connected with the meaning of Baptism. This is brought out further in the second account of creation by its emphasis on the theme of *naming.* Firstly, the beasts are brought to Adam to be named (2:19–20). We know that the act of naming was not understood in the ancient Hebrew tradition merely nominalistically, as in the attaching of an arbitrary label to something. We have already noted that the process of naming here represents something much more like appointing a place in the world, or even giving a mission — as Jesus named Simon the *Petrus* (rock) on which he would build his Church. What Adam is doing by naming the other creatures is quite simply *ruling,* as he was intended to do: ruling not for his own selfish aggrandizement, but simply in accordance with the reality of things and with the wisdom of God. This original state of justice or harmony between man and the rest of nature in paradise is sometimes glimpsed even in the fallen world, when in the presence of a person of special sanctity such as Saint Francis or Saint Cuthbert we are shown something of the friendship and obedience that the animals showed toward Adam.

There is a point that we need to consider. *What exactly are the "animals" to which Adam is giving names?* If we read Genesis as if it were written yesterday, by men with a modern mind-set, we naturally assume that the animals must be the primitive biological ancestors of the ones we know. That way lies the familiar conflict between creationists and evolutionists, both of whom in different ways read the Bible naively and with modern eyes. They come to different conclusions, but they make a similar mistake. The text was never intended to be read on one level only. We know that at least one of the beasts in the garden was not an animal in the modern sense at all, but an angel. According to tradition, the serpent in the story is that creature of God sometimes called the Archangel Lucifer. What if *all* the animals in the story were angels?

Charles Williams suggested something very like this in his novel, *The Place of the Lion*. "By the names that were the Ideas he called them, and the Ideas who are the Principles of everlasting creation heard him, the Principles of everlasting creation who are the Cherubim and Seraphim of the Eternal. In their animal manifestations, duly obedient to the single animal who was lord of the animals, they came" (from ch. 16). These living universals were intended to circle around the original man who was the "balance and pattern of all the Ideas."[4] If Williams is right, it is not just the animals of Eden that were angels; the essence of *every* animal species is an angel.

According to many ancient, apocryphal traditions (Christian, Jewish, and Muslim) God tested the angels at the beginning of time by informing them that it would henceforth be through Adam, the appointed mediator of creation, that they would have to give their praise. Their reaction to this command determined their fate. Some were prepared to humble themselves before Adam and were crowned with supernatural grace. Lucifer, on the other hand, refused to submit to a creature made from the dust and slime of the earth. If the animals of Genesis are indeed angels, what we have been given in the narrative of the naming of the animals is an account of the testing of the angels, told from the human point of view.

The importance of all this for Baptism lies in the implication that man is central to the cosmos, while the animals and angels are peripheral. Traditionally, this went along with the view that angels and animals are not merely beings in the world outside us; they also represent our own faculties, or aspects of human personality. Read in this way, the serpent becomes the ego or false self, a symbol of human pride rejecting or subverting the authority of the higher self that lives in harmony with God. As a result of this rebellion within, our personality is fragmented and dispersed, falling to a different and inferior level of existence (represented as the expulsion from Eden). The work of Baptism, which involves the re-naming of the self by the new Adam, is a work of healing and integration. Man can be once again the friend of angels, as we see after Jesus's own baptism in the Jordan and testing in the wilderness, when "angels came and waited on him" (Matt. 4:11).

Marriage. But the Bible's account of the sixth day does not only tell us about the essence of Baptism; it reveals a great deal about the sacrament of Marriage. According to our earlier meditations Marriage is the sacrament of the seventh day, but the connection between the sixth and seventh days is naturally very close. You could say that the sleep God imposes on Adam as he draws Eve from the man's side (Gen. 2:21) marks the transition between them — the movement from *Yesod* to *Malkuth*.

Marriage is the primordial sacrament. All the other sacraments are instituted by Christ as part of the new covenant (even if the grace they transmit can sometimes flow backwards through time). But Marriage was instituted in Eden. It forms the basis for the old covenant as well as the new, and though restored and renewed by Christ it already existed before he was born.

In recent years, no one has done more to reveal the depths of the biblical narrative than Pope John Paul II with his commentaries on the Book of Genesis, which have yielded a rich and complex theology of the body.[5] The Pope bases his reflections largely around the details of the second creation account. He reads this in the light of the fact that Jesus refers us back to this moment before the Fall when he restores the sacrament of Marriage to the way it should be (Matt. 19:3–9; Mark 10:1–12).

Adam's naming of the animals has revealed the fact that none is suitable as a partner for him. He is alone. The woman who is drawn out of him can be a partner because she is his equal, that is, equally central with him in relation to the animals and angels. "This at last is bone of my bones and flesh of my flesh; this one shall be called Woman [*ishshah*], for out of Man [*ish*] this one was taken" (Gen. 2:23). Woman reveals Adam's own nature to him. At the same time, she differs from him, and the nature of the difference is due primarily to fecundity. In this potential fecundity lies the divine image to which Genesis 1:27 refers: "So God created [the Adam] in his own image, in the image of God he created him; male and female he created them." In other words, the divine image is only perfected by dividing man into male and female in such a way that a third, a child, can be born of them. In this fact the Pope sees both an implicit revelation of the Trinity and a revelation of the nature of marriage as covenant, as well as a revelation of the nature of man as oriented to self-gift.

A covenant is a union in the flesh, which overcomes the separation between two individuals without destroying the difference between them. In fact it depends upon the difference between them. This is an image both of the Trinity and of the union between divine and human natures in the person of Christ — which extends itself into the union of Christ and the Church. But the covenantal union of marriage is not automatic or mechanical; it requires the deliberate pouring out of the one into the other (in a vow expressing mutual consent to self-gift, and in the sexual act). In this, too, something is revealed of the Trinity's nature as love — infinitely joyful, overflowing with an abundance of life.

Pope John Paul II makes much of the contrast between Genesis 2:25 and Genesis 3:10, the lack of shame before the Fall and the fear that the man and woman feel for the first time after the

Fall. Knowing they are naked, they hide themselves. This fear is partly a response to the emergence of lust, as a result of their separating themselves from God by disobedience. The initial purity and transparency of self-giving love has been compromised. Lust begins, however, not with the naked human body, but with the fruit. "So when the woman saw that the tree was good for food, and that it was a delight to the eyes, and that the tree was to be desired to make one wise, she took of its fruit and ate" (3:6). The spiritual dimension of these three temptations is due to the fact that they each represent a turning way from God, seeking fulfillment in *taking* instead of in *receiving*. The consequences of this threefold sin quickly become evident in the changed relationship of man and woman, now shaped by desire and power rather than mutual delight (3:16). The three temptations are only finally defeated by human nature in the person of the Son, when he rejects them in the wilderness after his baptism (Matt. 4:3–11), making possible the restoration of Marriage for those who join themselves to him in Baptism.

Notes

1. Essence and existence are technical terms in the writings of Saint Thomas Aquinas. The essence or "whatness" of a thing answers the question "What is it?" The existence or "thatness" of a thing answers the question, "Is it?" In the case of every created thing one can conceive that it might not exist, but God's essence is the same as his existence — it is "to be." God is not a thing in the world (even the first thing in the world), but the source of every possible world.

2. Schaya, *The Universal Meaning of the Kabbalah*, 15–16.

3. John Paul II, *The Theology of the Body*, 29. Only a few aspects of that metaphysical content can be dealt with here. Another, to which the Pope alludes, is the very important affirmation "God saw everything he had made, and behold, it was very good" (Gen. 1:31). Modern philosophy has divorced facts from values. Here the Bible affirms that the two are inseparable. Even the Fall does not revoke this affirmation of the essential goodness of creation.

4. In an article reproduced on the Second Spring website (*www.secondspring .co.uk/archive/monk.htm*), a monk of Holy Trinity Monastery writes: "None of the individuals of a species can account for the nature of the species as such. In order to explain the nature or form of any species, we are required to posit a cause which transcends the individuals of the species. Such a cause must contain the form of the species within it in a higher way without being itself part of the species. These are the spiritual substances or angels. The angels contain within themselves in a purely spiritual way the forms of things in the material world. . . . The causality of the angel of sparrows on the young sparrow is more intimate than even the sparrow's own mother. When the mother dies the sparrow continues to exist; but without the angel there would be no sparrows at all."

5. John Paul II, *The Theology of the Body*.

SEVEN

Reviving Mystagogy

This chapter serves as a kind of interim conclusion to this book of reflections on the Christian Way. But it will also jump off from these reflections in a practical direction.

Christianity is not a set of (more or less coherent) ideas. It is primarily a means of *salvation,* which is to say a method of integration — the integration of human with divine life. This does not mean that Christianity is merely an ethical system any more than it is an attempt to explain the world intellectually. The integration is a transformation; it goes much deeper than the exchanging of one pattern of habits for another. Christianity is declining in Europe largely because this essential interior dimension — the dimension in which we experience a living relationship with Jesus Christ — has been neglected.

I have written above about the sacraments of initiation. But often what happens after these sacraments are administered — after a new convert is received into full communion with the Church, for example, or after a young person is confirmed — is ... almost nothing. The new Christian is left to sink or swim in the parish. A shortage of priests or qualified spiritual directors means that such a person receives very little encouragement to journey deeper into the Christian mystery. They may not even be aware of the full richness of the spiritual resources that exist within the tradition of the Church, resources to help them grow in prayer and holiness and the knowledge of God.

Some people may find help within one of the new ecclesial movements or by attaching themselves as oblates to a monastery (and in fact there are many such opportunities if you look persistently for them), but many settle down into a routine Christianity that too often turns into a spiritual wasteland. As Arturo Elberti noted in 1998, "Every Christian, even a 'practicing' Christian, who does not have convictions rooted in conversion and in an adequate Christian initiation, is inevitably exposed to the danger of abandoning all religious practice, and with it faith itself."[1]

Baptism and Confirmation may be received only once. Christian initiation, however, is a continuing adventure, since the grace of these sacraments is the source of a new life of prayer that must grow or die. The need for ongoing catechesis in the mysteries of Christ and of the Church, a catechesis traditionally known as *mystagogia* ("initiation into the mysteries"), has been noted in Church circles for years. The modern revival of the ancient Rite of Christian Initiation for Adults (RCIA) by the Catholic Church in the 1960s was an attempt to recapture a sense of the initiatory power of the sacraments as it was experienced by the early Christians. There is a period of formal mystagogy at the end of the RCIA, which continues from Easter Sunday through Pentecost and then monthly for the remainder of the year. But it does not go nearly far enough. It certainly does not suffice to introduce the catechumen to the full richness of mystical theology. The Neo-Catechumenal Way (one of those movements I mentioned a moment ago) was specifically designed to offer a post-baptismal catechumenate. Its popularity confirms the need for such a process of re-initiation.

The Christian life is essentially creative. Indeed, one modern Russian Orthodox writer, Nicholas Berdyaev, has argued that the revelation of God to man must be complemented by a *revelation of man to God*, meaning the free, creative response that God yearns for us to produce on our own account. Other theologians have looked to the Blessed Virgin Mary as a model for our participation in God's plan as co-redeemers with Christ (this was the origin of a controversial proposal to give Mary the formal title of Co-Redemptrix). Yet too often we live our Christian lives mechanically, almost robotically. More shockingly still, the Church of practicing Christians is riddled with hypocrisy. It has become an all-too-human church rather than a Church of God. How our world would be transformed if more of us began to live the implications of the faith we profess!

If we are living only on the surface, if we have not been listening enough to the poets and visionaries, it is not surprising if our faith becomes like tumbleweed. It has no deep root in us. Coventry Patmore, the Victorian poet mentioned earlier in this book who was himself a convert to Catholicism, wrote in *Religio Poetae Etc.* (1893), "I do not see what is to become of popular Religion, parodied and discredited as Christianity is by the 'religions' of Atheists, Moralists, Formalists, Philanthropists, Scientists, and Sentimentalists, unless there can be infused into it some increased longing and capacity for real apprehension." He was right, and we have seen what has become of popular religion in our own day.

Hans Urs von Balthasar put it in more academic terms: according to him, integrating the act of perception back into our understanding of faith "is not only of theological and theoretical interest; it is a vital question for Christianity today, which can only commend itself to the surrounding world if it first regards itself as being worthy of belief. And it will only do this if faith, for Christians, does not first and last mean 'holding certain propositions to be true' which are incomprehensible to human reason and must be accepted only out of obedience to authority."[2] His books therefore explore the tradition of the "spiritual senses" — faith as a theological act of perception.

The fact is that in the face of modern skepticism, many people feel they can no longer accept the truths of faith simply on the Church's authority.[3] For them, especially, there has to be a way of *seeing into* the words of Scripture and the events of history, which reveals not merely a creed's logical consistency, not merely a moral code's merits, but the beauty that unites logic with life and truth with goodness. The eyes of faith will then open to reveal the radiance from within, a *gestalt* or form — Christ's form — that gives life to the words and events of salvation history. Not that faith and knowledge are the same thing, but they circle around each other, each leading into the other at a deeper level. And the result of this authentic Christian gnosis, its consummation, is not blind obedience but a *seeing love.*

One of the greatest of Christian teachers, who wrote under a pseudonym around five hundred years after the birth of Christ, is Dionysius the Areopagite,[4] sometimes called Saint Denys. His influence on Christian mysticism has been immeasurable, his orthodoxy assured by such admirers and interpreters as Maximus the Confessor in the East and Thomas Aquinas in the West. Denys is one of the all-time masters of mystagogy, and we would do well to take him as one of our guides in reviving the practice today.

What Dionysius did was divide the Christian Way into three phases — which he called *purification, illumination,* and *union* — and to link these to the three hierarchies of angels whose existence is attested by Scripture, who were thought to assist in each of the three phases.[5] The schema has been well tested over the centuries, and many saints have found it helpful. Purification is always needed at the beginning of an interior journey. Dionysius tells us that the angels of the lower hierarchy have a particular role and influence in the "active" life, that is, the life of the person who is in the process of becoming a servant of God. Angels of the middle hierarchy influence the "inner" life, by which we become sons in the Son. Angels of the final hierarchy influence and strengthen the "contemplative" life, through which we are divinized and become one with God by grace in the beatific vision. This final stage is what Saint John the Evangelist hints at when he writes (to those who have already some recognition of their co-sonship in God): "Beloved, we are God's children now [already]; it does not yet appear what we *shall be,* but we know that when he appears we shall be like him, for we shall see him as he is. And every one who thus hopes in him purifies himself as he is pure" (1 John 3:2–3).

So how might we try to live these three stages today? *Purification* corresponds to a path of gentle asceticism, refraining from luxuries, resisting consumerism, making more room for God in our lives, giving attention to liturgy, caring for others and offering hospitality, doing charitable works, healing wounds, repairing injustices, learning to pray. Added to this, *illumination* involves opening the eyes of faith, learning to read the books of nature and of Scripture, developing an inner study of metaphysics, music, and sacred art. Finally, *union* requires us to be consumed by love, to become our true selves through contemplation, even in the midst of action, and to be completely centered on the Other, in the likeness of the Trinity, in whatever way or form or mission the Lord decides.

An orthodox Christian will, of course, try to walk this triple path *within the Church,* that is, as part of the sacramental community whose underlying structure and dynamism we have explored in this book. But I can imagine a possible objection being raised by someone who has plunged into the mystical tradition of the Church, only to come up against a wall of human imperfection. This brings us back once more, by a slightly different route, to the central point.

Why is the Church so inadequate, so ugly, even (on occasion) so cruel? If even part of what I have said about the Church's sacramental nature is true, why is there not more evidence of holiness, of religious experience, among her members? Why do her priests and bishops so often seem to be little more than functionaries, lacking any real understanding of the great mysteries they administer? Why so much hypocrisy, so much spiritual failure, so much hardness of heart among the faithful? The more sensitive one becomes to the spiritual dimension of Christianity, the more keenly one feels this problem. Even in some parts of the Church where one sees health and growth, a close observer may on occasion become aware of deep-seated corruption, or resistance to the action of the Holy Spirit. This may express itself in sexual or emotional abuse, misogyny, or clericalism, or it may be much more subtle in the way it manifests itself outwardly. (But, by the way, detecting such failings is itself the occasion of a dangerous temptation — the temptation to judge, to denounce, to adopt a superior attitude.)

This constant failure of Christians is inevitable for the simple reason that the Church as she exists in time is *not a thing but a process*. At any given moment souls are rising or falling, responding to grace and resisting it. To the extent they resist the grace of God, the Church is in the process of dying in them. To the extent they respond to grace, the Church flickers back into life. And when a saint wins through to eternal life, even at the last possible moment (like the thief on the cross next to Jesus or the workers of the eleventh hour in the parable), a new member is added to the Church triumphant.

On earth, with our earthly eyes, we see the Church simply as an institution, a sociological group. We do not see her true members but only those who claim to belong to her. That is not always the same thing. Freed from the limitations of time, the Church is an organism, a person, a bride, because of the presence of Christ within her. Christ loves her, and she exists in each soul who joins her own will to his, becoming one flesh with him. This bride can be glimpsed in the Virgin Mary, where the Church's pattern and reality as a whole is most evident and concentrated. The invisible and cosmic Church *subsists*, nevertheless, in the imperfect institution we see. The two are indissolubly bound together, since it is through the institution that the mystical Church is continually coming into being.

With all this in mind, it is possible to read the following passage from Yves Congar with an open heart, without worrying that he may be idealizing a Church that does not actually exist. His words sum up the truth that this book has been attempting to communicate. I made some fairly detailed claims about a genetic code in the Christian religion that derives from the sevenfold structure of creation, and the corresponding sevenfold structure of its re-creation in Christ reflected in the sacraments. Behind this, I have suggested, lies the even deeper structure of the divine-human union in Christ, and beyond that what we might call the "inner triad" — namely the eternal Triunity of God. But the thrust of this book has not been towards a Gnostic analysis that would free us from the Church — quite the contrary. It has been at every point *toward communion,* toward our own deeper participation in those very mysteries. "In Jesus Christ the most perfect communion, the deepest and most holy communication have been given to us. By his Incarnation and his Easter, at the centre of . . . the line of time, the ultimate reality has entered human history to be the very means through which that reality is to be reached. Christ, who is the universe's Omega, has become our Alpha. He has instituted his apostles, his Church and his sacraments, precisely in order to join the Alpha to the Omega, his coming and his own personal Pasch to our Pasch with him. And so the Church is holy in depth, inwardly holy. Her sacraments bring a sanctity which is real. In her the means are of the same nature as the end, because Jesus Christ is the source of both end and means. The Holy Spirit is not present in and given to us only as a force, but as a holy Reality. It is the Spirit himself who is present and given, who dwells both in holy souls and in the Church. Sanctity means not merely to be consecrated to some work for God, it is inner communion and conformity with him."[6]

A Method for Exploring Mystagogy

Here are some suggestions of how you might try to implement the ideas in the final chapter of this book in your own parish or with your friends, by starting a course in the mystical teachings of the Christian tradition.

Mystagogy is the stage of exploratory catechesis that comes after apologetics, after evangelization, and after initiation (Baptism, Eucharist, and Confirmation). In the case of Catholics, familiarity with the *Catechism of the Catholic Church* is assumed, and an ongoing study of the *Catechism* is essential. A Catholic never outgrows the *Catechism*, but becomes capable of reading it at an ever-deeper level. Normally, by the time someone seeks mystagogy, primary initiation has taken place within the parish, and the sacraments (along with some form of daily prayer) have assumed a familiar and important place in everyday life. Daily Mass is recommended if practicable during the course, together with regular Confession and the use of some version of the Divine Office (the daily prayer of the Church).

Regular attendees would be expected to do some background reading and private study between sessions, following the outlines or suggestions provided by the convenor. (These might include some of the books listed in the following bibliography, but there are many Christian classics that might be appropriate, depending on the group's preferences and needs. In the UK, the Catholic Truth Society is publishing a series of booklets to provide some parish resources for mystagogy.)

The course's aim is to help bring the student into a closer personal relationship with Jesus Christ through the Church. The guiding principle is the *beauty of holiness* — holiness as the unity of beauty, truth, and goodness.

A convenor or instructor should facilitate each series of sessions. The course should start with invited guests only; for practical reasons the sessions are not automatically open to all. Sessions are intended for Christians who are seeking a deeper experience of prayer or of the Church's mystical traditions.

Meetings should be in a friendly environment — in a private home or adjoining a chapel — and would involve (1) prayer, (2) social time (cookie time, or tea if in England), (3) a talk and/or discussion. No more than half an hour is necessary for each section. Meetings should take place once every week or two weeks if possible for the duration of the course, which can take place at any time of year depending on the circumstances of the group.

The convenor does not aim to usurp the role of priest, nor offer spiritual direction in the traditional sense of that phrase. The group should not become dependent on the convenor's personality or skills, but must function on the basis of a common purpose, a growing friendship in the faith, and within the guiding framework of course materials provided. The convenor's role is to remind the students constantly of the living presence in their midst of Christ as the teacher, and the in-dwelling and life-giving Holy Spirit.

The convenor's responsibilities are to invite the participants, to provide the venue and the structure for the sessions, to enable the group to follow an organized course of instruction, to

introduce and close each session, to support the group in the use
of traditional spiritual practices (Lord's Prayer, Rosary, Icons,
Divine Office, and so on), to help students to evaluate their experience with these practices, and to assist students in moving
on to other things when the course no longer serves their needs.

Awake, O sleeper,
and arise from the dead,
and Christ shall give you light.

Ephesians 5:14

Notes

1. Pontifical Council for the Laity, *Rediscovering Baptism.* Elberti's chapter
is an informed survey of the whole question of a "post-baptismal catechesis."
2. Von Balthasar, *The Glory of the Lord,* 140.
3. Faith, as we have seen, is a gift of God, a grace, an infused virtue. It
takes the form of an accepting response to the authority of the self-revealing
God. Our obedience in faith is to the Word who is the revelation of the Father,
and the Word is made present to us through the mediation of the community
founded on that Word (the Church) and in-formed by the Holy Spirit. Yet
there is always a need both for rational preambles to faith, which prepare the
ground for it (largely by removing obstacles), and for a subsequent process
of discerning exploration if the faith is to remain alive and active in us.
4. Termed "Pseudo" because his writings were not in fact those of the
contemporary of Saint Paul, the Areopagite mentioned in Acts 17:34, in whose
name he was writing.
5. The three sets of three are (beginning with the lowest), Angels,
Archangels, and Principalities; Powers, Virtues, and Dominions; Thrones,
Cherubim, and Seraphim.
6. Congar, *The Mystery of the Temple,* 202–3.

Bibliography

Titles marked with an asterisk (*) are recommended as basic texts helpful for beginning a mystagogy course. The translation of the Bible most frequently consulted for the purposes of this book is the Revised Standard Version. The King James Version was used in chapter 6.

Anon. [V. Tomberg] *Meditations on the Tarot: A Journey into Christian Hermeticism.* Amity, NY: Amity House, 1985.

Ayo, Nicholas. *The Lord's Prayer.* Notre Dame, IN: University of Notre Dame Press, 1992.

Bonaventure, Saint. *Breviloquium.* London: B. Herder, 1946.

————. *Collations on the Ten Commandments.* Works of Saint Bonaventure, vol. 6. St. Bonaventure, NY: Franciscan Institute, 1995.

Borella, Jean. *Guénonian Esoterism and Christian Mystery.* Hillsdale, NY: Sophia Perennis, 2004.

* ————. *The Secret of the Christian Way: A Contemplative Ascent through the Writings of Jean Borella.* Ed. G. John Champoux. Albany: State University of New York Press, 2001.

Bouyer, Louis. *Liturgical Piety.* Notre Dame, IN: University of Notre Dame Press, 1954.

Cabasilas, Nicholas. *A Commentary on the Divine Liturgy.* London: SPCK, 1960.

Caldecott, Stratford. *Catholic Social Teaching: A Way In.* Rev. ed. London: Catholic Truth Society, 2003.

* *Catechism of the Catholic Church.* UK revised edition. London: Geoffrey Chapman, 1999.

Champoux, G. John. *The Way to the Heavenly Father: A Contemplative Telling of the Lord's Prayer.* Hillsdale, NY: Sophia Perennis, forthcoming.

Chesterton, G. K. *Heretics* (1905). In *The Collected Works of G. K. Chesterton.* Vol. 1. San Francisco: Ignatius Press, 1986.

Clark, Stephen B. *Catholics and the Eucharist: A Scriptural Introduction.* Ann Arbor, MI: Servant Publications, 2000.

Claudel, Paul. *The Essence of the Bible.* New York: Philosophical Library, 1957.

* Clément, Olivier. *The Roots of Christian Mysticism: Text and Commentary.* London: New City, 1993.

The Seven Sacraments

Congar, Yves M.-J., OP. *The Mystery of the Temple* or *The Manner of God's Presence to His Creatures from Genesis to the Apocalypse*. London: Burns & Oates, 1962.

* Corbon, Jean. *The Wellspring of Worship*. San Francisco: Ignatius Press, 2005.

Daniélou, Jean. *The Angels and Their Mission*. Westminster, MD: Newman Press, 1957.

———. *The Bible and the Liturgy*. Notre Dame, IN: University of Notre Dame Press, 1956.

———. *From Shadows to Reality: Studies in the Biblical Typology of the Fathers*. London: Burns & Oates, 1960.

de Lubac, Henri. *Medieval Exegesis*. Vol. I: *The Four Senses of Scripture*. Grand Rapids, MI: Wm. B. Eerdmans, 1998.

Gaudoin-Parker, Michael L. *Heart in Pilgrimage: Meditating Christian Spirituality in the Light of the Eucharistic Prayer*. New York: Alba House, 1994.

———. *Hymn of Freedom: Celebrating and Living the Eucharist*. Edinburgh: T. & T. Clark, 1997.

———. *The Real Presence through the Ages: Jesus Adored in the Sacrament of the Altar*. New York: Alba House, 1993.

Grabowski, John S. "Person: Substance and Relation," *Communio* (Spring 1995): 139–63.

Guardini, Romano. *Meditations before Mass*. Manchester, NH: Sophia Institute Press, 1993.

Haffner, Paul. *The Sacramental Mystery*. Leominster: Gracewing, 1999.

Hahn, Scott. *A Father Who Keeps His Promises*. Ann Arbor, MI: Servant Publications, 1998.

———. *First Comes Love: Finding Your Family in the Church and the Trinity*. London: Darton, Longman & Todd, 2002.

———. *Letter and Spirit*. New York: Doubleday, 2005.

Hopper, Vincent Foster. *Medieval Number Symbolism: Its Sources, Meaning, and Influence on Thought and Expression*. Mineola, NY: Dover, 2000.

John Paul II, Pope. *The Theology of the Body: Human Love in the Divine Plan*. Boston: Pauline, 1997.

Lewis, C. S. *The Abolition of Man*. New York: Macmillan, 1947.

McPartlan, Paul. *Sacrament of Salvation: An Introduction to Eucharistic Ecclesiology*. Edinburgh: T. & T. Clark, 1995.

Miller, Paula Jane, FSE. *Marriage: The Sacrament of Divine-Human Communion*. Vol. 1: *A Commentary on St. Bonaventure's Breviloquium*. Quincy, IL: Franciscan Press, 1996.

Maximus, Saint. *Maximus the Confessor: Selected Writings*. Trans. George C. Berthold. New York: Paulist Press, 1985.

Bibliography

* Mazza, Enrico. *Mystagogy: A Theology of Liturgy in the Patristic Age.* New York: Pueblo Publishing Co., 1989.

Mensch, James Richard. *The Beginning of the Gospel According to Saint John: Philosophical Reflections.* New York: Peter Lang, 1992.

Patmore, Coventry. *Religio Poetae Etc.* London: George Bell & Sons, 1893.

Pieper, Josef. *Leisure, The Basis of Culture.* South Bend, IN: St. Augustine's Press, 1998.

Pinckaers, Servais, OP. *The Sources of Christian Ethics.* Washington, DC: Catholic University of America Press, 1995.

Pontifical Council for the Laity. *Rediscovering Baptism.* Vatican City: Vatican Press, 1998.

Pseudo-Dionysius. *Pseudo-Dionysius: The Complete Works.* Trans. Colm Luibheid. New York: Paulist Press, 1987.

Randolph, Francis. *Know Him in the Breaking of the Bread: A Guide to the Mass.* San Francisco: Ignatius Press, 1994.

Ratzinger, Joseph. *A New Song to the Lord: Faith in Christ and Liturgy Today.* New York: Crossroad, 1997

———. *Introduction to Christianity.* San Francisco: Ignatius Press, 1990.

* ———. *The Spirit of the Liturgy.* San Francisco: Ignatius Press, 2000.

———, Heinz Shürmann, and Hans Urs von Balthasar. *Principles of Christian Morality.* San Francisco: Ignatius Press, 1996.

Riley, Patrick. *Civilizing Sex: On Chastity and the Common Good.* Edinburgh: T. & T. Clark, 2000.

Schaya, Leo. *The Universal Meaning of the Kabbalah.* London: Allen & Unwin, 1971.

Schmemann, Alexander. *For the Life of the World: Sacraments and Orthodoxy.* Crestwood, NY: St. Vladimir's Seminary Press, 2000.

* Sheen, Fulton J. *The Seven Capital Sins.* New York: Alba House, 2001.

Stein, Edith. *The Science of the Cross.* Washington, DC: ICS Publications, 2002.

Tomberg, Valentin. *Covenant of the Heart.* Rockport, MA: Element Books, 1992.

Tavard, George H. *Transiency and Permanence: The Nature of Theology according to St. Bonaventure.* St. Bonaventure, NY: Franciscan Institute, 1954.

von Balthasar, H. U. *First Glance at Adrienne von Speyr.* San Francisco: Ignatius Press, 1981.

———. *The Glory of the Lord: A Theological Aesthetics.* Vol. 1: *Seeing the Form.* San Francisco: Ignatius Press, 1982.

von Speyr, Adrienne. *Confession.* San Francisco: Ignatius Press, 1985.

* ———. *The Cross: Word and Sacrament.* San Francisco: Ignatius Press, 1983.

———. *The Gates of Eternal Life.* San Francisco: Ignatius Press, 1983.

———. *The Holy Mass.* San Francisco: Ignatius Press, 1999

Wood, Susan K. *Spiritual Exegesis and the Church in the Theology of Henri de Lubac.* Grand Rapids, MI: Wm. B. Eerdmans, 1998.

Yarnold, Edward, SJ. *The Awe-Inspiring Rites of Initiation: The Origins of the RCIA.* Edinburgh: T. & T. Clark, 1994.

Zizioulas, John D. *Being as Communion: Studies in Personhood and the Church.* Crestwood, NY: St. Vladimir's Seminary Press, 1985.

Online

The St. Paul Center for Biblical Theology, containing rich resources for the study of Scripture and tradition:
www.salvationhistory.com

The work of Jean Corbon, *The Wellspring of Worship:*
http://rumkatkilise.org/wellsprings.htm

The complete text of Romano Guardini, *Sacred Signs:*
www.ewtn.com/library/liturgy/sacrsign.txt

The Veil, contemplating the Christian mysteries:
www.theveil.net

The Interpretation of the Bible in the Church, an important survey document by the Pontifical Biblical Commission:
www.ewtn.com/library/curia/pbcinter.htm

Second Spring, containing articles and links on many related subjects:
www.secondspring.co.uk

About the Author

Stratford Caldecott is currently the Director of the Oxford office of the G. K. Chesterton Institute for Faith & Culture, and the editor of the journal *Second Spring* (along with the associated website, *www.secondspring.co.uk*). He is also on the editorial boards of *The Chesterton Review* and the American edition of the theological and cultural review *Communio,* for both of which he writes regularly, having lived in both the United States and Britain. The author of *The Power of the Ring: The Spiritual Vision Behind the Lord of the Rings* and *Catholic Social Teaching: A Way In,* and the editor of books on the Catholic historian Christopher Dawson and on the liturgical reform movement in the Catholic Church, he has written and published widely on Christian apologetics, theology, and cultural themes in magazines and newspapers on both sides of the Atlantic, including *Touchstone, Parabola,* and the *National Catholic Register.* He has taught at Plater College in Oxford and at the Newman Institute in Ireland.

Caldecott studied Philosophy and Psychology at Oxford University. He is married to the writer Léonie Caldecott; they have three children and live in the Cotswolds near Oxford.

A Word from the Editor

It goes without saying that being an editor of non-fiction books is the most consistent way of obtaining a free education in a grand array of subjects, especially if those books are written by very intelligent and disciplined writers who become experts in their respective fields. I have often thought that my theological education has been going on for thirty years past my actual master's degree. So I am the beneficiary of continuing education in my field just by doing my job consistently and paying attention to what my writers are saying and thinking.

In this specific case with this specific book I feel like I have received a whole year of classroom instruction but in the form of one small book. Stratford has a way of saying a lot in few words. And he has a way of shedding new light on a topic in a way that keeps surprising his readers, and me. That is even more impressive when you think about how many books and authors have tackled the subject of the Christian sacraments. There are literally hundreds of contemporary books on this topic. You can scroll through one of the online bookstores and find that those hundreds of books are substantial and written for all ages and for all levels of education. When you think of this subject and its importance down through the ages, then you can easily imagine that there have been thousands of books on this topic by the greatest minds in the church.

And still this book is unique and compelling. It is written with a certain flair for intellectual clarity and creativity. It makes what is old, new again. It informs while edifying. It actually makes me feel like I can say with candor and authenticity, "If you are going to read one book on the Sacraments this year then this is the book you should read." You might think an editor would say that about every book he or she publishes. But we, of all people, know that even as much as we love every book we edit and publish, there are classics in every field and we can't publish a classic every time we make a decision to allow a book to see the light of day in the world of books and publishing. Since reading the first draft of this volume I felt like I was in the presence of a carefully wrought and clearly written little classic on the subject. I kept wanting to read it again and make sure I had learned and remembered everything there was to learn and remember. Stratford's *Seven Sacraments* will have the same effect on many readers, I am willing to predict. And even though when you are reading about a mystery you really can't capture all of it, by its very nature, you will have a sense of why these mysteries of the Christian faith are so important and why they are so powerful. In accomplishing that with this little book Stratford has served all of us and the whole church.

Roy M. Carlisle
Senior Editor

Index of Subjects

Adam, 6, 8, 59, 61, 63, 70,
118–22
angels, 30, 35, 67, 108, 117–20,
123, 127–28, 133
animals, 59, 105, 117–20
**Anointing, 8, 19, 30, 46–47,
49, 75–78, 106, 114**
Apostles, 38, 130

**Baptism, 6, 8, 11, 19, 21, 27,
34, 37–41, 56–60, 110,
115, 118–20**
beatitudes, 91–94. *See also*
Sermon on the Mount
Bible. *See* Scripture
body, theology of the, 117,
120–22

catechesis, 12, 125
Catechism of the Catholic Church,
5, 8, 10, 22, 38, 44, 85, 89,
131
charity. *See* love
chastity, 43–44
Christ, Jesus, 5–6, 7–10, 14,
23, 38, 52–78, 87–88, 124,
127, 132

Christ, Jesus (*continued*)
ascension of, 8, 15, 41, 66
cross of, 11, 18, 19, 21, 26,
29, 38, 45, 60, 63, 71
incarnation of (hypostatic
union), 2, 7, 11, 15–16, 18,
34, 71, 121, 130
passion of, 19, 29, 59
Redeemer, 18, 74, 115
resurrection of, 26, 40, 76
temptations of, 50, 74–75, 83
See also God, Last Supper,
last words
Church, 6–9, 17–18, 31, 33,
38, 47, 52–53, 56, 60, 65,
67, 69, 77–78, 96, 105, 118,
121, 124–25, 128–31, 133
teaching authority of, 23,
127
Church Fathers, 1, 3–4, 16–17,
55, 57, 117
clericalism, 129
Commandments (Decalogue),
85–95, 101–2, 112–13
Communion, Holy, 7, 26, 30.
See also Eucharist
Confession. *See* Reconciliation

Index of Names

Bibliographical references are not included in this index except where texts have been quoted or paraphrased. For biblical names see the Index of Subjects.

Of Related Interest

Stratford Caldecott
THE POWER OF THE RING
The Spiritual Vision Behind the Lord of the Rings

J. R. R. Tolkien, author of *The Lord of the Rings*, often said that his great mythic saga made no sense without the rich Catholic faith and imagery at its heart. In *The Power of the Ring*, Stratford Caldecott, a beloved scholar and author, offers the first definitive book on this key to understanding the themes of quest, love, devotion, forgiveness, and healing.

0-8245-2277-X, $16.95, paperback

Check your local bookstore for availability.
To order directly from the publisher,
please call 1-800-707-0670 for Customer Service
or visit our website at *www.cpcbooks.com.*
For catalog orders, please send your request to the address below.

THE CROSSROAD PUBLISHING COMPANY
16 Penn Plaza, Suite 1550
New York, NY 10001

All prices subject to change.

crossroad